# In-Style Accent TABLES™

Designs by Sandi Hauanio

HOUSE of WHITE BIRCHES
PUBLISHERS SINCE 1947

# CONTENTS

DESIGN INTRODUCTION ............................ 3

SIMPLE SIDE TABLE ...................... 12

ELEGANT PEDESTAL TABLE ....................... 18

MAHOGANY & WALNUT END TABLE ..... 26

CHERRY HALL TABLE ................................ 34

CIRCULAR COFFEE TABLE ........................ 42

GEOMETRIC ILLUSIONS TABLE ................. 48

WALNUT & WENGE COFFEE TABLE ........ 56

# SANDI HAUANIO

Sandi Hauanio started woodworking in 1990 while attending Herron School of Art in Indiana. She earned a Bachelor of Fine Art in Furniture Design in 1994 and continued her education at Herron for an extra year. During her last year in school she entered and won the prestigious Design Emphasis Award for Design Creativity at the International Woodworking Fair in Atlanta, Ga.

Over the years, Sandi has expanded her knowledge of woodworking by exploring new techniques and designing new and different furniture and sculpture pieces. She is an artist and her medium is wood.

Sandi is a founding member and current vice president of the local women's woodworking guild and has recently become a member of The Furniture Society. She also teaches woodworking classes at her local art center.

# DESIGN INTRODUCTION

Furniture design does not have to be complicated, as Sandi Hauanio demonstrates in her first book, *In-Style Accent Tables*. Design, she says, is all about personal taste. There is no "wrong" way to design. In step-by-step fashion, she guides the reader through the design process, from concept and thumbnail sketches to finished drawings and materials lists. Get started with these basics and soon you'll be designing your own projects.

The thought of building a piece of furniture that you have designed yourself can be both exciting and intimidating. Without formal training, you may think you do not have enough knowledge about design to create an original piece of furniture. This is simply not true.

Design is about personal taste. If you can look at an object and decide what you do and do not like about it, you can design. Take a look at a piece of furniture. What do you think? Do you like it? Is it pleasing to your eye? What would you change about it? Would you make it taller, shorter, wider? Would you choose a completely different type of wood altogether?

With the right tools and a willingness to explore, anyone can design something of their own. Remember, there is no "wrong" way to design. Give yourself permission to let loose and be creative.

The table has been chosen as a first design project because most tables generally have the same components. From pedestal tables to end tables, almost all tables consist of a

## DESIGN INTRODUCTION

tabletop, legs and some type of support system.

There are seven table plans provided in this book. Their proportions can be changed, elements added or taken away, and components can be mixed and matched. Whether you choose to use the plans exactly or change them in some way or another, this book can help give you the skills you need to get started with the design. Good luck, and enjoy!

### TOOLS OF THE TRADE
**Visual references**
Visual references are things that help stimulate your creative juices. They can be anything from magazines, books and woodworking plans to architectural elements on buildings and bridges or fences and windows.

One of my favorite things to do is to visit the bookstore and flip through all of the interior design and architecture magazines. Any of the visually stimulating art magazines will do. You may see a texture or shape in a ceramic magazine or a color or pattern in a textile magazine. You never know what is going to pique your interest or how you can incorporate it into your furniture design.

Woodworking books are great to look at, too. Sometimes seeing a certain kind of joinery can inspire you to create a design based on the use of that joint. You can gain new ideas and even new ways to use old ideas by doing a little "visual research."

**Sketchbooks**
An integral part of the design process is sketching, so getting a sketchbook you like is very important. I like to do my initial sketching either in an unlined hardcover sketchbook or even just a college rule notebook, something that has a binder so that I don't lose my sketches.

I have saved my sketchbooks over the years. Sometimes, if I have a hard time coming up with new designs, I will get out my old sketchbooks and flip through the pages. It's almost like flipping through all your old photographs. It brings back memories of where a design of something I've already made had its beginnings and how the design evolved from its initial sketches.

**Grid paper**
One of the best things you can get to aid your design process is grid paper. Grid paper is paper that is printed with squares of equal size over the entire page. It is sold in office supply stores and art supply stores, and I have even found grid

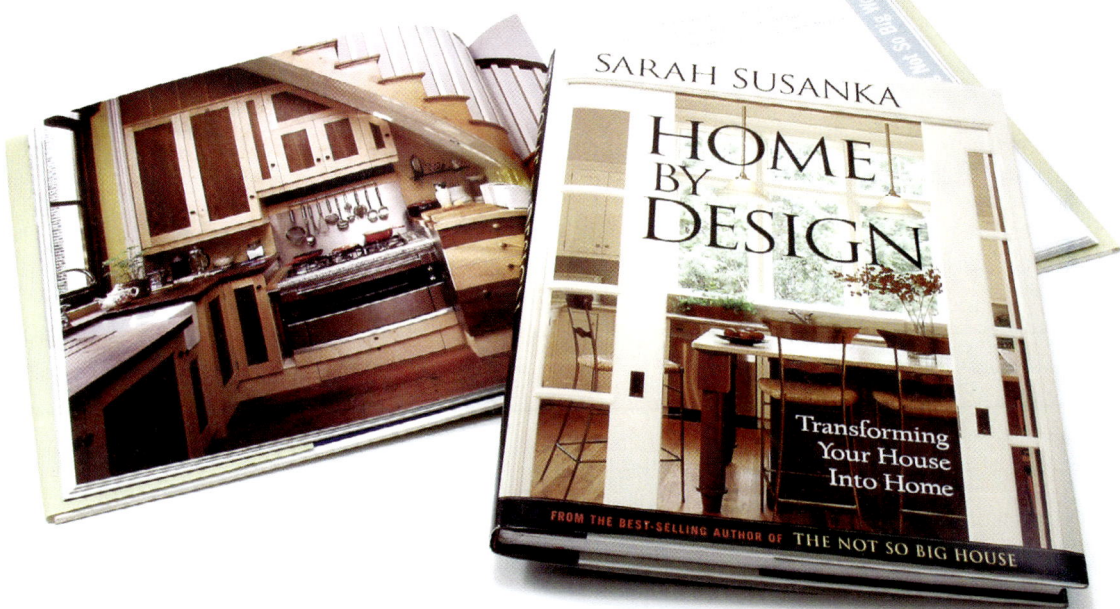

# DESIGN INTRODUCTION

paper on my Microsoft Works computer program.

Grid paper comes with a variety of square sizes. If I know I will be working on a design for something large, I will get grid paper with a smaller sized square so that I will be able to fit the design onto one page.

The reason grid paper is so helpful is that you don't need a drafting board and a T square just to get a reasonable idea of what your design will look like. Using the squares as your measurements, you can draw out your ideas quickly and accurately to scale. (Scale drawings will be discussed later.) It is easy to see the proportions of your design and where you might need to make changes. Depending on the size of your table, you can fit several versions of one design on the same page.

## Mechanical pencils

Mechanical pencils are pencils that have replaceable lead. They come with different lead sizes and the lead is available in different degrees of hardness. The best mechanical pencil to use is one that has a metal tip. When using a ruler, the metal tip runs along the side of your straight edge, protecting the lead. This prevents the lead from breaking and keeps the thickness of your drawing lines consistent. I like to use a .05 mm pencil with a 5 mm HB pencil lead and a white Mars Plastic Staedtler eraser. Colored erasers seem to really smudge your drawing and eat up your paper, making it rough to draw over.

## Straight edges

You can use anything with a straight edge to draw a line, but I prefer a steel ruler. I have a 6-inch steel rule. It is thicker than a regular metal ruler, which makes it easier to use. Your pencil won't slip and run over the top of the ruler while you are drawing. The other thing I like about using a small ruler is that its length doesn't interfere with drawing. I don't always draw at a desk or table; sometimes I draw in bed or while sitting on the couch. A longer ruler tends to catch or snag on things while you are trying to draw—like clothes or blankets. Smaller rulers are also more convenient to carry around. You never know when you'll have a great idea or see something you don't want to forget and you never know when the mood to draw will strike.

## French curves

French curves are highly useful when you want to draw any kind of a curved line. They are generally sold in sets of three: two small ones and one large. The large one is the one I find most useful. The curves are usually made of a clear plastic. You can use the French curve while you

## DESIGN INTRODUCTION

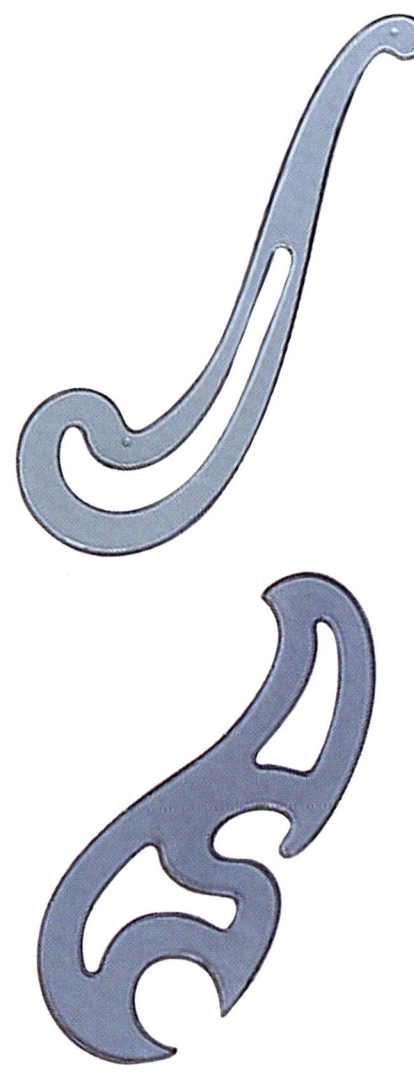

are designing and they can also be used when making a full-size template for something like a curved leg or apron.

Most of the time you are just using part of the curve, which means you have a large variety of different radii available in each of the French curves. To repeat a curve from one leg to the next, I make a mark right on the plastic of where the top of the leg starts. I draw the first leg, make a mark on the curve and then draw the second leg, positioning the mark on the curve with the top of the leg. This makes it easy to make each leg look the same.

There are other templates available that have lots of different size ovals and circles. These can be found at drafting supply stores.

### Other curves

You can also use what is called an adjustable curve or a flexible curve. Both of these are available in a 24-inch length, and can be used for making larger templates. Either one of these can be found in woodworking specialty stores or art and drafting supply stores.

### BASIC DESIGN PROCESS

Designing is a process and like any other process, designs take shape through a series of steps. These steps don't really have a specific order, so feel free to go through the process in a way that fits your needs and moods. Everyone's reason for creating is different. What one person gets out of the whole process can be, and usually is, completely different from another person. I am generally building something for the experience itself, rather than necessity, and that definitely plays a large part in the outcome of my designs.

I give myself complete freedom to explore many different aspects of woodworking. Sometimes a piece may be about the joinery, other times about a specific pattern or type of wood. What drives me to design and build furniture is the challenge. The process of creating is a never-ending, ever-changing and always-interesting learning experience.

In the world of woodworking, there is always more than one way to get the job done. Design is the part of that process that determines the way in which you choose to do that.

### Thumbnail sketches

Whether you are designing with a specific project in mind or just something for fun, most designs start off with an initial idea. Sometimes I get an idea and think about it for quite awhile before I ever put anything down on paper. Other times I have a thought and immediately draw it out. I generally start out with thumbnail sketches. These are sketches that are usually rather small in scale and don't have much detail.

Thumbnail sketches are quick thoughts, generally consisting of just a few lines—a doodle. These help you to see a basic shape, the curve of a leg or shape of a tabletop quickly. You may do 20 or so quick sketches and choose to further develop only one of the ideas. The point of a thumbnail sketch is to get a whole lot of ideas down on paper quickly. This can help loosen you up and start to stimulate your creative juices. There is not a lot of critical thinking involved in this step; no analyzing is involved until you are completely finished.

Once you have a page or two of thumbnail sketches, take a good look at what you've drawn. Are there one or two ideas that you are drawn to more than the others? Is there a common detail or shape that runs through several of the sketches? Is there something that interests you in one of the sketches, something that you want to explore further and develop? Sometimes, if I am just sketching, it may just be a line or shape that interests me. I may not have already decided what the item is going to be. For example, a shape you may have wanted to incorporate as perhaps a table leg may, instead, become the shape of the apron. Maybe you had decided to make a table but the shapes you keep drawing lend themselves more appropriately to a chair.

**Sketches**

Once you find something interesting, something you want to develop further, you can start doing a more serious series of sketches—sketches that focus in on the detail you are developing.

These sketches can be done on the same kind of paper that you used with the thumbnail sketches. This is the part of the design process when you start to consider

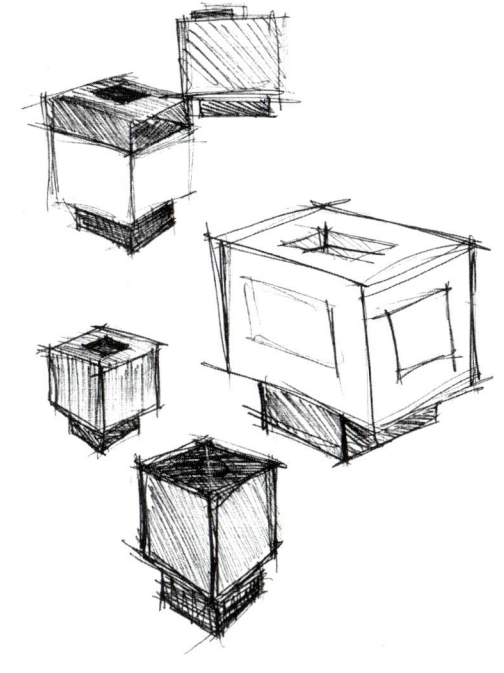

## DESIGN INTRODUCTION

more than just the aesthetic issues. At this point, your design is still going to go through changes.

## DETERMINING FACTORS OF DESIGN

### Functions
There are many factors that will help determine the final outcome of a design. The first set of concerns is mostly functional. First of all, what type of table are you building? Where will the table sit? Is it in a corner or is it at the end of your couch? Will it be mostly a decorative piece or will it serve a more specific purpose? Is it just going to have an alarm clock on it, or some magazines, or will people be putting food and beverages on it? Does the table need to also have some sort of storage ability? These types of practical concerns will be some of the most important factors of your design.

### Aesthetics
Once the functional concerns have been defined, the second set of concerns is usually more about aesthetics. Do you want the table to really stand apart from the other things you have in the room, like an accent piece, or do you need it to blend with the rest of the décor?

Take a hall table, for example. They are often the first thing you see when you walk into your house. Functionally, the table may only serve as a place where you drop your keys and mail, but aesthetically, it's the first thing you see when you come home every day. Because the functional needs are so minor, you are much more free to explore the aesthetic side of the design.

If you are building a table with more functional concerns—for example, a coffee table—it may be more important that it fit in with the rest of the room. The height, for example, will depend on the height of your couch. Look around the room. Are there any details you can incorporate into your design? Maybe it's the color of the couch that you want to complement, or there may be a pattern in a rug that you want to repeat in your table.

### Skill level
Skill level also plays a very large part in the outcome of your design. If you are a beginner, your options will be a little more limited, in both knowledge and tools, than if you are an advanced woodworker. The more you learn about woodworking, the more complicated your designs may become.

I learned woodworking at an art school. I had the luxury of a fully equipped shop and the benefit of working with great teachers. I knew my time there was limited, though, and took advantage of the situation. I made it a point to learn a new technique, use a new tool or try a new type of joinery technique with every project I made. My woodworking knowledge and skill level was always a key factor in my designs.

So, once you feel you have some basic skills down, move on to something more challenging. There is never just one way to put something together and never just one solution in woodworking. Expand your knowledge and try something new. This will help to expand your design skills, too.

**Tools**

You need tools to do woodworking—it's a fact. For most of us, accumulating tools is a gradual process. We can't afford to go out and buy enough tools to equip a full shop. So, work with what you have and maybe buy a new tool with each new project.

Your designs will definitely be influenced by what kinds of tools you own. The area in which the tool plays the biggest part is in what kind of joinery you will be using. You may be limited in your choices if you have a limited amount of tools. Don't be shy, though, in trying new ways of joining things together. There are all kinds of gadgets to help you.

**Scale drawings**

Once you feel like you have a good idea for a design, the next step is to make a scale drawing. Scale drawings are used to get an accurate picture of a piece of furniture. When I say accurate, I am referring to proportionately accurate. Full-scale, actual-size drawings are not only time consuming but, depending on the size of the piece, may be virtually impossible to fit on even a large sheet of paper. They require using a drafting board, triangle and T-square.

Full-scale drawings, for the most part, just aren't necessary to get an accurate picture of your design. This is where our grid paper is irreplaceable. Because grid paper comes in all different sizes, you can choose the size accordingly. Ideally, we want to be able to fit a front view, side view and top view of our table on one page. With all of our information and measurements on one page, it makes it much easier to view. This also makes it much easier to use when you are in your workshop. Thus, if you are working on a large design, you will want to do one of two things: Either choose a grid with smaller squares, or assign the measurement of each square a larger size. For example, you can choose that each square represents 2 inches, 1½ inches, 1 inch, ½ inch, etc. The larger the measurement you assign to the squares, the larger drawing you can fit onto the page. I will usually rough out the basic dimensions to see if all three views will fit before I start drawing. This way I can choose the appropriate size squares.

**Working drawings**

Once you get the drawings laid out on your grid paper, it is time to put in the measurements. Fig. 1 is an example of a completed working drawing. It has all the measurements and information that we will need to build the table. The drawing will help us make a clear and concise cut list which, in turn, allows us to figure out our materials list.

Adding dimensions to a drawing is very simple. Switching to a .7 mm pencil is sometimes helpful, as the lead is harder. This allows a difference in line weight between the drawing and the measurements. It is not absolutely necessary, but it does help you to decipher between the lines of your drawing and the lines of your measurements.

The first thing to do when preparing a working drawing is to determine the scale of the grid paper, for example, one square equals 1 inch (see sample scale drawing on page 10). Label each view (top, front, side) or detail (leg/apron detail) as needed. Label measurements in ascending order so that overall dimensions can be clearly seen and understood. The front view of the table in the sample drawing on page 10 is a good example. The width of the leg (2 inches) is indicated by arrows beneath the leg and the distance between the legs (16 inches) is indicated by arrows between the legs. The total width of the table (20 inches) is indicated by arrows that encompass the widths of the legs and the distance between them.

You should always use arrows or

DESIGN INTRODUCTION

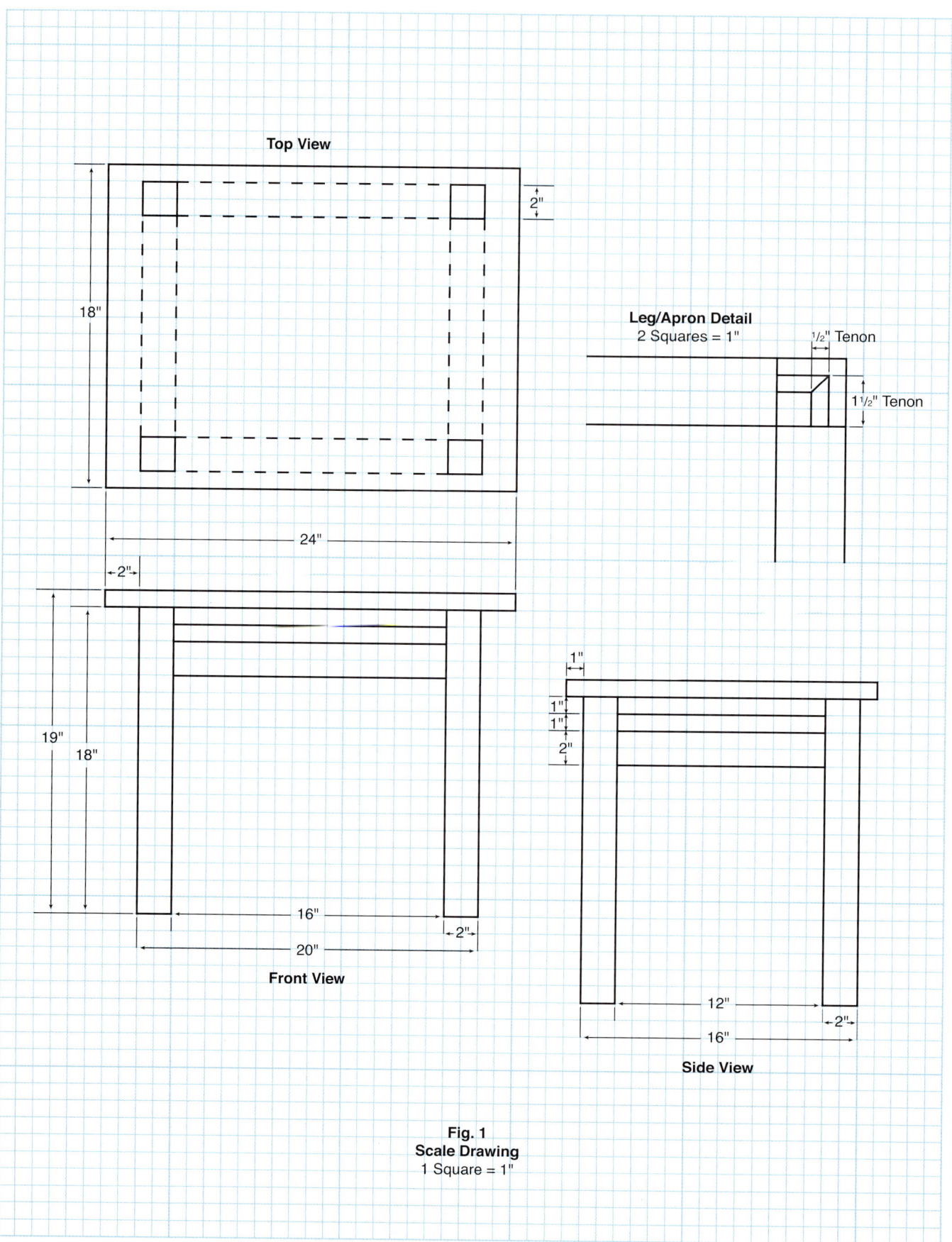

Fig. 1
Scale Drawing
1 Square = 1"

perhaps a short diagonal mark at the end of each line. This allows you to see exactly what part of the design the measurement is referring to.

Any measurements that you will need but cannot actually see should be drawn with a dashed line. Refer to the top view drawing. The only measurement that we still need is the width of the table apron because we haven't been able to see it from any other view. Since this is a necessary piece of information, we definitely can't leave it out. Drawing the structure with dashed lines lets us know that the table top is a solid piece, but there is information below the top that we need.

Usually there are details that you may need to draw out in order to understand and see more clearly. In our example, I decided to draw a detail of the mortise and tenon joint, where the apron connects to the legs. Now I see that I need to add an extra 3 inches to the length of each apron piece. If I hadn't done this extra detail drawing, I might have forgotten to add the extra length. If you are tackling something a little more challenging than usual, it's very helpful to do a full-scale drawing of some of these details. Any part of the design that you can't see clearly in your head can be more easily understood if you are able to see it on paper.

**Materials list**

Once you have completed drawing your design and laying in the measurements, it's time to create a materials list. Of course, you should check and double check your measurements first. Once you are sure you have all the correct information, make a list of parts including their measurements.

### SAMPLE MATERIALS LIST

**Tabletop**
1x24x18 inches

**Legs**
2x2-inch stock: 6 feet

**Apron**
*The lengths of the apron pieces include the tenons.*
1x2-inch stock: 6 feet
2x2-inch stock: 6 feet

**Nominal lumber**

Keep in mind, these measurements are nominal measurements. In general, lumber is sold based on rough dimensions. In other words, when a lumberyard purchases lumber, they buy it rough. This means the tree has been sliced into planks of different thicknesses, depending on how the mill wants to sell it. The tree is sliced up using something like a chainsaw or a really wide band saw blade, leaving the planks with a really rough cut.

The lumberyard can either sell the lumber to you as is—rough—or they can clean and straighten the lumber by jointing and planing it, and sell it to you at a higher price, already surfaced.

Regardless, you will still be charged for the lumber at its nominal measurement. So, for our table, the legs that we have drawn as 2x2 inches will actually be about 1¾ inches thick; our apron pieces will actually be about ¾x1¾ inches thick; and our tabletop will be about ¾ inch thick.

If you do the surfacing yourself and pick nice, straight boards, you will probably be closer to the larger dimensions listed. If you buy your wood already surfaced it will be closer to the smaller dimensions listed. Regardless, the only part of our design that it may change is the overall size of the tabletop. Planning ahead, we will cut the tabletop last to make up for any changes.

Once you have the working drawing done, it's time to get started on the building of the table. Keep your working drawing in the shop with you so that there is no guessing involved. You will have all the information you need at your fingertips. A well-thought-out design can save lots of money and time by helping you make fewer mistakes. ✱

# SIMPLE SIDE TABLE

The base of this table is so easy to build, you can spend a bit more time getting creative with the top!

### PROJECT SIZE
13½x24¾x12¾ inches

### TOOLS
- Miter saw
- Combination square
- Clamps greater than 13-inch bite
- Drill with ¼-inch bit and #8 countersink bit
- Self-centering doweling jig
- Flush cut saw (optional)

### SUPPLIES
- ¾x¾ walnut*: 24 feet
- ¾x4x12¾-inch maple* (for tabletop)
- ¾x6x9½-inch maple* (for tabletop)
- ¾x8x6¾-inch maple* (for tabletop)
- ¾x3¾x1½-inch maple* (for tabletop)
- 26 #8x1½-inch wood (or drywall) screws
- Six #8x1-inch wood (or drywall) screws
- ⅜-inch walnut plugs
- Wood sanding block
- 120- and 180- grit sandpaper
- Yellow wood glue
- ¼x1½-inch dowel pins
- Clear wood finish

*Measurements given are actual, not nominal. Standard nominal lumber will need to be ripped and/or planed to size.

*Note: A dust mask is essential when working with woods such as mahogany and walnut as the sawdust from such woods is toxic and can do serious and long-term damage to your lungs.*

### CUTTING

1 From ¾x¾-inch walnut, cut eight 12-inch lengths (B) for base frame and shelf, five 11¼-inch lengths (A) for base frame, and four 24-inch lengths (C) for legs.

### ASSEMBLE & FINISH
**Bottom shelf**

1 Select the two ¾x¾x11¼-inch walnut pieces (A) for the bottom shelf rails. Place them side by side with the ends flush and mark at the following measurements: 1, 1¾, 2¾, 3½, 4½, 5¼, 6, 6¾, 7¾, 8½, 9½, 10¼. Square across and mark so both 11¼-inch boards are identical; extend the lines so the top, bottom and outside

## SIMPLE SIDE TABLE

# ASSEMBLY DIAGRAM

**SIMPLE SIDE TABLE CUTTING CHART**

| P | T | W | L | # |
|---|---|---|---|---|
| A | ¾" | ¾" | 11¼" | 5 |
| B | ¾" | ¾" | 12" | 8 |
| C | ¾" | ¾" | 24" | 4 |
| D | ¾" | 4" | 12¾" | 1 |
| E | ¾" | 6" | 9½" | 1 |
| F | ¾" | 8" | 6¾" | 1 |
| G | ¾" | 3¾" | 1½" | 1 |

## SIMPLE SIDE TABLE

edges of each piece are marked.

**2** Draw an "X" from corner to corner between the following marks on the outside of both boards: 1 and 1¾, 2¾ and 3½, 4½ and 5¼, 6 and 6¾, 7¾ and 8½, 9½ and 10¼ (Fig. 1). The center of the "X" is the drill point.

**3** Place the two 11¼-inch pieces on a flat surface with two of the 12-inch pieces (B) between. Align the 12-inch pieces in the last pair of marks of each side: the 1 to 1¾-inch space and the 9½ to 10¼-inch space. Place clamps so the ends of the 12-inch pieces are accessible; clamp frame together. Be sure all pieces are flush.

**4** Using the #8 countersink and drill bit, drill a hole through the outside of the 11¼-inch slats into the ends of the 12-inch slats. Attach with 1½-inch wood screws. Once the outside pieces are attached, remove the clamps and attach the remaining four 12-inch slats in the same manner (Fig. 2).

**Fig. 1
Bottom Shelf A Slats**

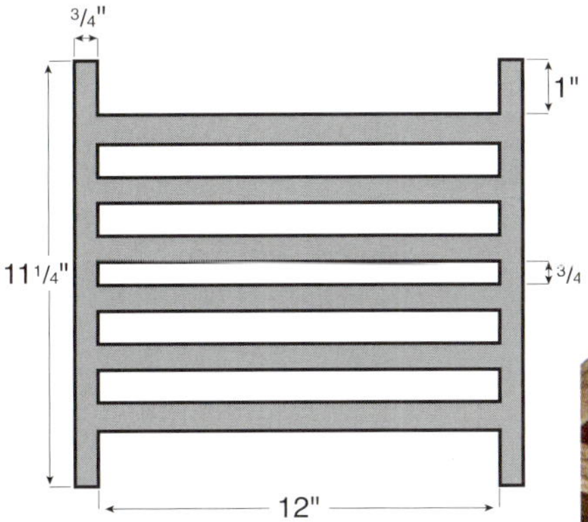

View of Underside of Bottom Shelf

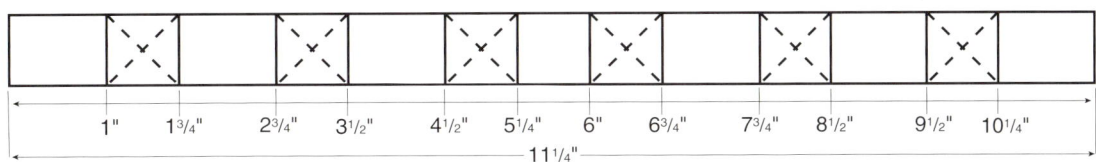

**Fig. 2
Bottom Shelf Top View**
Attach 12" slats to 11¼" slats.

## SIMPLE SIDE TABLE

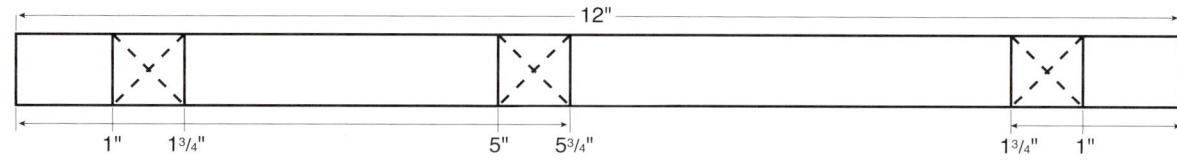

**Fig. 3**
Mark and drill 12" slats.

### Top support

**1** For side slats, refer to Fig. 3 to mark two 12-inch walnut pieces (B) as in Step 1 of bottom shelf.

**2** Butt two 11¼-inch slats (A) into the two 12-inch side slats 1 inch in from each end; clamp in place. Be sure all edges are flush. Drill through the 12-inch side slats to attach the two 11¼-inch slats. Attach the third 11¼-inch slat, beginning at 5 inches from one end. This middle slat will not be centered.

### Legs

**1** Mark all four sides of each leg (C) at 6 inches and 6¾ inches up from the bottom. Draw an "X" on the outside edges as instructed previously.

**2** Using the countersink and drill bit, attach the legs (C) to the ends of the 11¼-inch side slats (A) of the bottom shelf with 1½-inch screws.

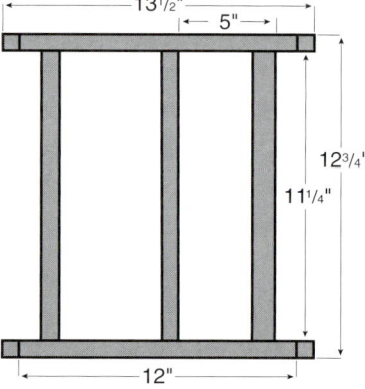

**Fig. 4**
**Top Support Top View**
Butt ends of 12" slats to legs.

**3** Stand the legs upright and attach the top support side slats (B) to the legs, butting slats into legs with top edges flush (Fig. 4); attach, using countersunk 1½-inch screws as in previous steps. *Note: The slats in the top support will run perpendicular to the slats in the bottom shelf.*

**4** Fill countersunk holes with ⅜-inch plugs, making sure the grain of the plug runs in the same direction as the grain of the legs and slats. Trim the plugs using a flush cut saw, or sand flush.

**View of Underside of Top Support & Top**

SIMPLE SIDE TABLE

### Tabletop

1. Referring to Fig. 5, lay out the pieces of the tabletop for correct placement. Clamp together and mark placement of the dowels as indicated.

2. Using the dowel centering jig and ¼-inch bit, drill all the holes for the dowels a little over ¾ inches deep.

3. Dry fit the pieces together. Once you are satisfied with the fit, disassemble.

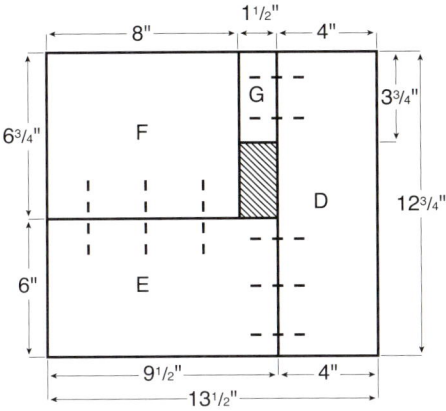

**Fig. 5**
Assemble pieces as shown.
Place dowels as indicated
by dashed lines.

### FINISH

1. Sand the top and bottom surfaces of the four tabletop pieces (D, E, F, G), slightly rounding over the edges.

2. Apply finish to the tabletop and base prior to assembly, following manufacturer's instructions.

### FINAL ASSEMBLY

1. Glue, dowel (¼x1½-inch), and clamp top pieces D and E together.

2. Glue, dowel and clamp together piece G to piece D.

3. Glue, dowel and clamp piece F to piece E, gluing the edges between F and G at the same time; clamp and wipe away any excess glue. Be sure there are no glue runs or drips. Let dry.

4. Place the tabletop upside down on work surface. Center the base upside down on top of it. Attach, using countersunk #8x1-inch wood screws through the three slats. ✽

# ELEGANT PEDESTAL TABLE

A Danish Modern influence can be seen in this unique two-toned piece.

**PROJECT SIZE**
15x33⅝x13 inches

**TOOLS**
- Miter saw
- Table saw with dado blade
- Combination square
- Band saw or jigsaw (or surform, microplane and rasps)
- Drill press (or drill) with ½-inch and ¾-inch Forstner or spade bits
- ½-inch or smaller chisel
- Random orbit sander
- Two or more 12-inch clamps

**SUPPLIES**
- 1½x1½-inch mahogany*: two 10-foot lengths, and one 4-foot length
- 1⅜x12-inch tiger maple*: 14 inches
- 1x1-inch mahogany*: 4 feet
- 80-, 100- and 220-grit sandpaper
- Yellow wood glue
- Eight 1⅝-inch drywall screws
- Four figure-8 tabletop fasteners
- Clear wood finish

*Measurements given are actual, not nominal. Standard nominal lumber will need to be ripped and/or planed to size.*

## PROJECT NOTES

This project has been done in tiger maple and mahogany, but any combination of woods, such as an oak top and cherry base, would be appealing. Perhaps even an oak top and cherry base. Be creative and make this a table you will value for a lifetime.

A dust mask it is essential when working with woods such as mahogany and walnut as the sawdust from such woods is toxic and can do serious and long-term damage to your lungs.

If 1⅜x12x14-inch tiger maple is not available, glue up several narrower boards until the 12-inch width is reached. Alternate end grains and apply glue to the edges of the boards. Clamp together and let dry.

## CUTTING

1. From 1½x1½-inch mahogany, cut four 32¼-inch lengths (A) for legs, four 13¾-inch lengths (B) for front and back aprons, and four 11¾-inch lengths (C) for side aprons.

2. With the table saw, cut 1⅜x12x14-inch tiger maple to 1⅜x11½x13½ inches (D) for tabletop.

3. From 1x1-inch mahogany, cut two 12-inch lengths (E) and two 10-inch lengths (F) for tabletop cleats.

### Leg Curves

1. Mark the two sides of each leg (A) that will face outward on the table. Set all of the legs together in a row, making sure the tops are flush, and make a mark 10¼-inches up from the bottom on one leg. Using the combination square and a pencil, draw a line accross the remaining legs (Fig 1A).

2. Turn the legs so the other outside edge is up and mark the 10¼-inch mark across all four legs. There should now be a 10¼-inch mark on both outside edges of all four legs.

ELEGANT PEDESTAL TABLE

## ASSEMBLY DIAGRAM

| P | T | W | L | # |
|---|---|---|---|---|
| **ELEGANT PEDESTAL TABLE CUTTING CHART** | | | | |
| A | 1½" | 1½" | 32¼" | 4 |
| B | 1½" | 1½" | 13¾" | 4 |
| C | 1½" | 1½" | 11¾" | 4 |
| D | 1⅜" | 11½" | 13½" | 1 |
| E | 1" | 1" | 12" | 2 |
| F | 1" | 1" | 10" | 2 |

ELEGANT PEDESTAL TABLE

**Elegant Pedestal Table Leg Curve Template**

1½"
¾"
10¼"

Pencil line for top of curved template. Carry the line around all four sides of each leg at 10¼-inches.

**3** Using the template provided, transfer lines for the curve of the legs. **Note:** *It may be easier to make a copy and flip it for a mirror image as each side of each leg will have the cut curving from the inside toward the outside bottom of the leg. For reference, the only corner that will remain intact is the corner joining the two surfaces marked as the outside of the legs.* Place the template so the straight edge of the template is along the corner that is shared by the two outside edges of the leg, and the top of the template is at the 10¼-inch line. Tape it in place and mark the curve. Do this until you have marked two cuts on all four legs (Figs. 1B and 1C). On the very bottom of the leg, draw a reference line connecting the ends of the leg curve lines. This will aid in cutting the curve.

**4** Cut the curves on each leg. You may do this with the Sur-Form, microplane, band saw or jigsaw by cutting just short of the line and sanding to the line with the 80- or 100-grit sandpaper. Do not remove material past the reference lines (bottom of leg and at 10¼ inches up).

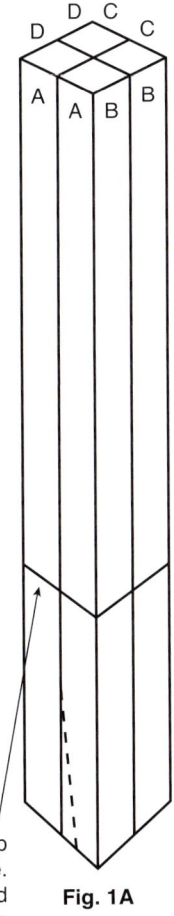

Fig. 1A

Fig. 1B

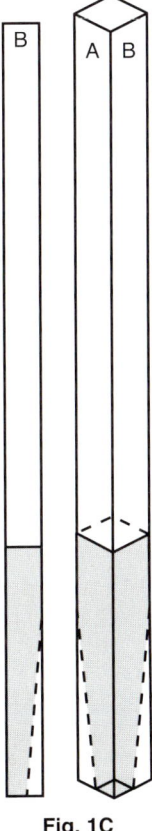

Fig. 1C

**Leg Curves**

ELEGANT PEDESTAL TABLE

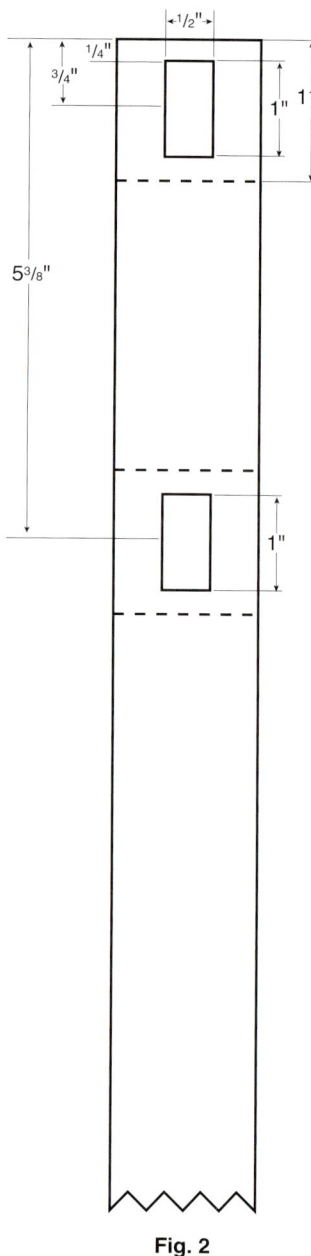

Fig. 2
Leg Mortises

## Leg mortises

**1** Mortises will be ½ inch wide, 1 inch high and ⅞ inch deep, centered horizontally in the width of the leg, with two mortises on each inside edge of each leg (A). The top mortise will be centered vertically at ¾ inch from the top of the leg. The bottom mortise will be centered vertically at 5⅜ inches from the top of the leg (Fig. 2). Mark the rectangle for each mortise on the inside edge of each leg, then draw a vertical line in the center of each. This will help center the drill bit.

**2** Set the drill press to drill ⅞-inch into the leg. Set the fence so

ELEGANT PEDESTAL TABLE

that the point of the drill bit hits the center of the width of the leg. The first hole will be lined up so the bottom edge of the bit just touches the bottom of the mortise outline. The second hole will be lined up so the top edge of the drill bit touches the top of the mortise outline. Cut each of the top mortises first by drilling these two holes into the legs in all eight places (Fig. 2). Repeat the process for the bottom mortises. Chisel out waste. This will result in 16 mortises ½ inch (width of the drill bit) by 1 inch (two consecutive drill bit widths) by ⅞ inch (depth of the drilled holes).

**Apron tenons**

1 Determine which edge will be to the outside of all eight apron pieces (B, C) and mark them accordingly.

2 Set the dado blade on the table saw to cut ¹³⁄₁₆-inch wide and ¼ inch deep. Set the table saw fence ⅞-inches from the edge of the blade furthest from the fence.

*Note: Before cutting the apron tenons, practice the following steps on a scrap piece of wood of the same dimension. Test fit this practice piece into the mortises for fit. If the end result is not a tenon that is ½x1x⅞-inches, or if it doesn't fit the mortises, then make the necessary adjustments before you actually cut the apron pieces. Make the tenon fit the mortises, not vice versa.*

3 Referring to Fig. 3, cut the top of each apron piece on all four sides, making sure the body of that piece stays flat on the table saw (apron tenon side view). Raise the blade to ½ inch and cut the eight aprons on the inside and outside edges only (apron tenon top view).

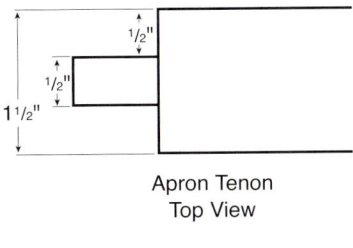

Apron Tenon
Top View

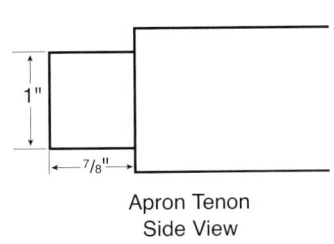

Apron Tenon
Side View

**Fig. 3**

4 Using the miter saw, cut a 45-degree miter on each of the tenons, with the long point to the outside of the apron piece and the short point to the inside (Fig. 4).

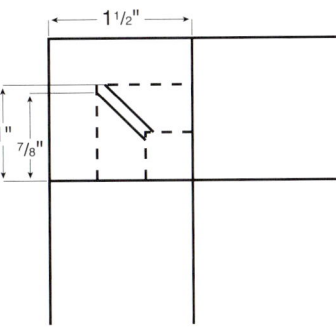

**Fig. 4**
Top View of Aprons and Leg
Mortise and Tenon

## ELEGANT PEDESTAL TABLE

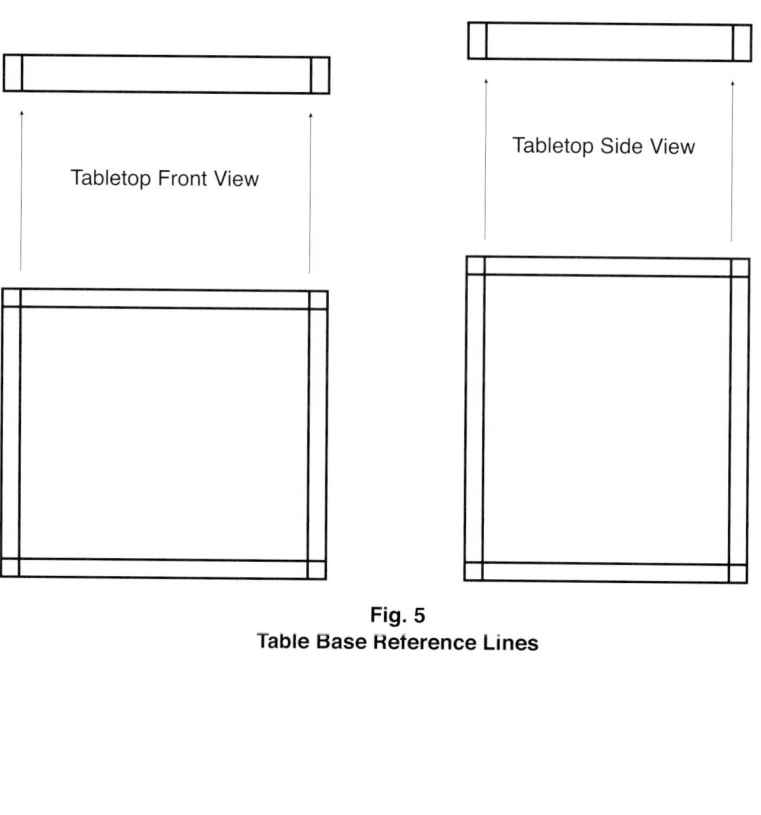

**Fig. 5**
Table Base Reference Lines

**Fig. 6**
Bottom of Tabletop
Reference Lines

**Fig. 7**
Bottom of Tabletop
Bevel Lines

## ASSEMBLE & FINISH

**1** Assemble the legs (A) and aprons (B, C) without glue to make sure everything fits properly. If the tenons are too tight, trim them with a knife. If they are too loose, use shims to make them more snug.

**2** Sand all table base edges with 220-grit sandpaper, being careful not to alter the mortises or tenons in any way. (If a random orbit sander is not available to you, and you are hand sanding, sand with the grain so surfaces are not scratched.)

**3** Glue and clamp table base together. ***Note:*** *Use scrap blocks of wood to protect the surface to be finished from the pressure of the clamps.*

**4** Center the tabletop (D) on the table base and clamp in place. Mark the inside of the base frame onto the bottom of the tabletop. Unclamp the top and transfer these lines to the 1⅜-inch thickness of the tabletop (Fig. 5).

**5** Draw a line all the way around on the tabletop edges ¼-inch down from the top (Fig. 6). On the ends, draw a bevel line from the bottom line of the base frame to this ¼-inch line at both sides of each corner (Fig. 7).

**6** Set the table saw angle and fence to cut this bevel angle. Cut the two opposite sides, then reset the fence and cut the two remaining sides. Check for fit, then sand and finish the tabletop.

**7** With the miter saw, miter the ends of the four tabletop cleats

ELEGANT PEDESTAL TABLE

(E, F) creating a frame. Glue the cleats on the inside top of the table base about 1/16-inch below the top of the base and attach with countersunk 1 5/8-inch drywall screws, one at each end of each cleat (Fig. 8).

**8** Using the 3/4-inch Forstner bit, drill a hole 1/16-inch deep in the center of each of the cleats for the figure-8 fasteners. Using the screws provided, install the larger side of the figure-8 fasteners into these 3/4-inch holes.

**9** Set the tabletop in place and predrill the holes for the figure-8 fastener screws; attach the top.

**10** Do touch-up sanding as necessary, then apply finish following manufacturer's instructions. ❋

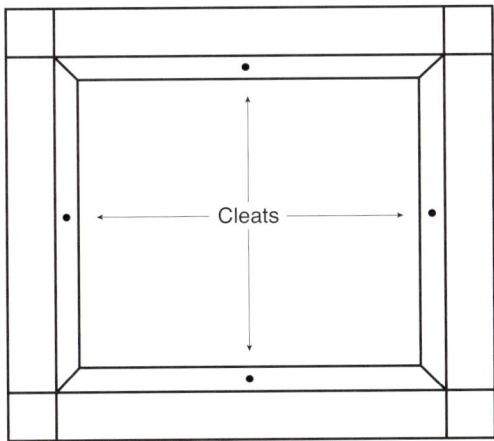

**Fig. 8**
Top View of Table Base

# MAHOGANY & WALNUT END TABLE

Mahogany and walnut combine with stunning results in this small end table. Walnut plugs add design interest while hiding fasteners from view.

### PROJECT SIZE
15x15⅝x21⅝ inches

### TOOLS
- Miter saw
- Table saw with dado blades
- Combination square
- Self-centering doweling jig
- Assorted clamps
- Drill with ¼-inch bit and #8 countersink bit
- Flush cut saw (optional)

### SUPPLIES
- ¾x5-inch mahogany*: 48 inches
- ¾x1¹¹⁄₁₆-inch walnut*: 24 inches
- ¾x1⁵⁄₁₆-inch walnut*: 12 inches
- 1x1-inch mahogany*: 14 feet
- ¾x9⅛-inch mahogany*: 12 inches
- ¼x1½-inch wood dowel pins
- Yellow wood glue
- Sandpaper in assorted grits
- Cyanoacrylate glue
- ⅜-inch walnut plugs
- #8x1½-inch wood (or drywall) screws
- #8x2-inch wood (or drywall) screws
- Clear wood finish

*Measurements given are actual, not nominal. Standard nominal lumber will need to be ripped and/or planed to size.

**Note:** *A dust mask is essential when working with woods such as mahogany and walnut as the sawdust from such woods is toxic and can do serious and long-term damage to your lungs.*

## CUTTING
**Note:** *Use miter saw throughout.*

1. From ¾x5-inch mahogany, cut two 15-inch lengths (A) and two 5-inch lengths (B) for tabletop.

2. From ¾x1¹¹⁄₁₆-inch walnut, cut two 5-inch lengths (C), two 3⅝-inch lengths (D) and two 1¾-inch lengths (G) for tabletop inlay.

3. From ¾x1⁵⁄₁₆-inch walnut, cut two 3⅝-inch lengths (E) and two 1¾-inch lengths (F) for tabletop inlay.

4. From 1x1 mahogany, cut four 20⅞-inch lengths (I) for legs, four 13-inch lengths (H) for crosspieces, four 2-inch lengths (J) for tabletop supports and four 1-inch lengths (L) for bottom shelf supports.

5. Cut ¾x9⅛-inch mahogany to 9⅛-inch length (K) for bottom shelf.

## ASSEMBLE
### Tabletop

1. Referring to Fig. 1, lay out mahogany tabletop pieces (A, B).
**Note:** *The grain of the two 5x5-inch (B) pieces will run perpendicular to the grain of the two 5x15-inch (A) pieces.* Be sure all outside edges are flush; using a square, mark the dowel locations as indicated by dashed lines. With the self-centering doweling jig and a ¼-inch bit, drill each dowel hole ¾-inch deep.

2. Dry-fit tabletop together, then disassemble. Assemble with glue and dowel pins, then clamp together until dry. Remove clamps and sand

MAHOGANY & WALNUT END TABLE

# ASSEMBLY DIAGRAM

**MAHOGANY & WALNUT CUTTING CHART**

| P | T | W | L | # |
|---|---|---|---|---|
| A | ¾" | 5" | 15" | 2 |
| B | ¾" | 5" | 5" | 2 |
| C | ¾" | 11/16" | 5" | 2 |
| D | ¾" | 11/16" | 3⅝" | 2 |
| E | ¾" | 15/16" | 3⅝" | 2 |
| F | ¾" | 15/16" | 1¾" | 2 |
| G | ¾" | 11/16" | 1¾" | 2 |
| H | 1" | 1" | 13" | 4 |
| I | 1" | 1" | 20⅞" | 4 |
| J | 1" | 1" | 2" | 4 |
| K | ¾" | 9⅛" | 9⅛" | 1 |
| L | 1" | 1" | 1" | 4 |

MAHOGANY & WALNUT END TABLE

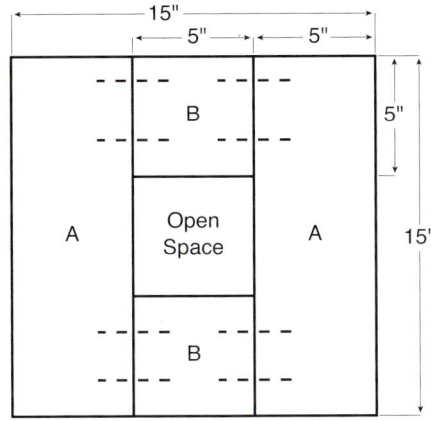

**Fig. 1**
Lay out tabletop pieces and mark placement of dowels.

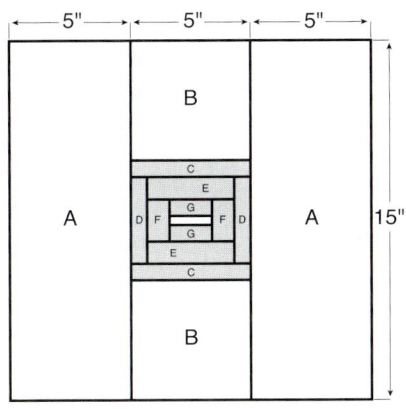

**Fig. 2**
Trial-fit inlay pieces before gluing in place.

top, bottom and outside edges, slightly rounding over top edges.

**3** Sand tops of walnut tabletop inlay pieces (C, D, E, F, G), slightly rounding over top edges. Trial-fit each piece, trim as needed, then glue in place with cyanoacrylate glue in the following order (Fig. 2): two ¾x11⁄16x5-inch pieces (C) against the 5x5-inch outer pieces (B); two ¾x11⁄16x3⅝-inch pieces (D) against the 5x15-inch pieces (A); two ¾x15⁄16x3⅝-inch pieces (E) against the first inlay pieces (C); two ¾x15⁄16x1¾-inch pieces (F) against the second inlay pieces (D); two ¾x11⁄16x1¾-inch pieces (G) against the third inlay pieces (E).

## Cross supports

*Notes: The four crosspieces will become two sets of supports half-lapped together in the middle. Since the crosspieces are 1x1 inch, the half-lap cut will also be 1 inch wide, but only ½ inch deep.*

## MAHOGANY & WALNUT END TABLE

*Practice on a scrap piece of wood that is 13 inches long and 1 inch or more thick. Be sure the practice cuts are correct before cutting the crosspieces.*

1. Set the dado blade on the table saw to cut ½ inch deep and 9/16 inch wide; set the fence so the cut begins 6 inches from the end of the board. Make one pass with the first crosspiece (H).

2. Turn the crosspiece so the opposite end is against the fence and the same side is being cut. Make the second pass. The end result should be a nice clean ½-inch deep by 1-inch-wide groove (Fig. 3).

3. Repeat steps 1 and 2 for each remaining crosspiece (H). Sand all four pieces, avoiding the joints.

### Table base

1. Determine which side of each leg (I) will face outward. Measuring from the bottom of the leg, make a mark on the outside at 4 inches and one at 5 inches. Draw a line across each mark; draw an X between these lines (Fig. 4). This will be the drill point.

2. Measure down from the top of each leg (I) and mark at 2 inches and 3 inches; draw a line across each mark and draw an X between the lines to find the drill point.

3. Place one leg (I) on its side on a flat surface with one crosspiece (H) on the inside of the leg at the

**Fig. 3**
Cut a half-lap joint in the center of each crosspiece.

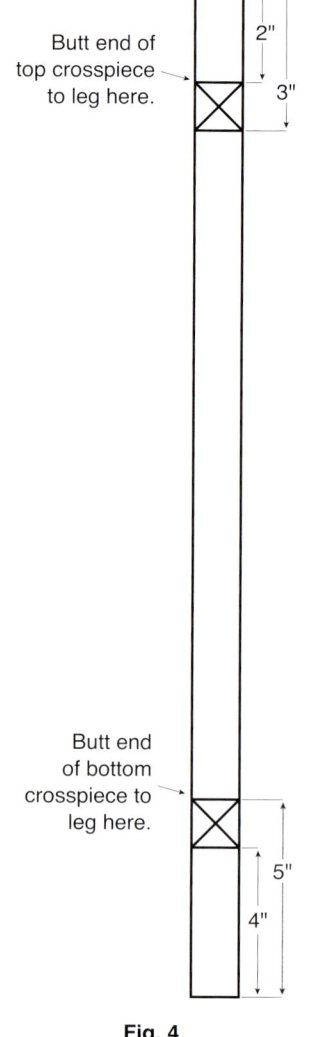

**Fig. 4**
Mark placement of top and bottom crosspieces on each leg.

bottom X. Make sure the half-lap groove is toward the bottom. Clamp together. Drill and countersink a hole through the leg into the crosspiece; attach with a #8x2-inch wood or drywall screw.

4 Lay out and attach the upper crosspiece (H) to the same leg (I) in the same manner (half-lap groove up). Attach the opposite leg to the crosspieces.

5 Attach the remaining bottom crosspiece (H), with the half-lap groove toward the bottom, to the remaining two legs following the same procedure as in steps 3 and 4.

6 Assemble the base unit by gluing and clamping together the half-lap joints. Secure the remaining top crosspiece (H) with glue and clamps by predrilling and countersinking the holes through the legs as in previous steps.

## Tabletop

1 Turn the tabletop on its face; mark the bottom for leg and support placement as follows (Fig. 5): Measure in from the end and mark 7 inches and 8 inches on each side. Draw a line across the width of the table top at each mark and up the sides. From each of the four sides of the tabletop, measure toward the center along the parallel lines and mark 1 inch, 2½ inches and 3½ inches. Draw an X in each square as shown.

2 At each X, drill straight through the tabletop from the bottom to the top.

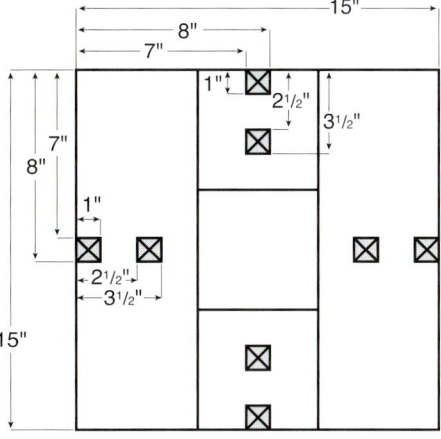

**Fig. 5**
Mark placement of legs and tabletop supports.

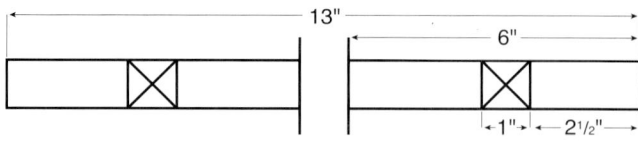

**Fig. 6**
Mark placement of tabletop supports on top crosspieces.

3 Turn the tabletop back over and set it on the base assembly; clamp in place and drill and countersink through the holes for the table legs. The legs should be flush with the outside edge of the tabletop and centered along each side. Secure the tabletop to the legs with 1½-inch screws.

### Tabletop supports

1 Lay the table upside down. Measuring from the outside of each leg, mark the bottom of the top crosspieces (H) at 2½ inches and 3½ inches from each end. Draw lines and mark the X (Fig. 6).

2 Place the 2-inch tabletop support pieces (J) between the top crosspiece and the tabletop at each of the X's just marked. Holding the support in place, drill and countersink a hole through the crosspieces at the X, then attach the support with a 2-inch screw. Repeat for the other three support pieces.

3 Set the table upright again and drill and countersink through the holes you already made through the top for the supports. Secure the supports from the top with 1½-inch screws.

### Bottom shelf

1 Make sure the bottom shelf (K) is ¾x9⅛x9⅛-inches. Sand the top, bottom and edges, slightly rounding the top edges.

2 Mark 4⁹⁄₁₆ inches and 5⁹⁄₁₆ inches across each side. Draw lines at those marks across the bottom of the shelf. At each set of parallel lines, measure toward the center from the edge and mark ⅜ inch and 1⅜ inches. Mark the X in each resulting square on both the top and bottom of bottom shelf (Fig. 7).

3 Drill from the bottom of the shelf through to the top at the marked X's as in step 2 of the tabletop.

4 Measuring from the outside of each leg, mark the top of the bottom crosspieces (H) at 3½ inches and 4½ inches from each end as in step 1 of tabletop supports. Draw lines and mark the X.

5 Place each 1-inch support (L) on X marks of both crosspieces. Place the shelf on the supports and clamp in place. Countersink the holes already made in the shelf for the supports. Secure the supports

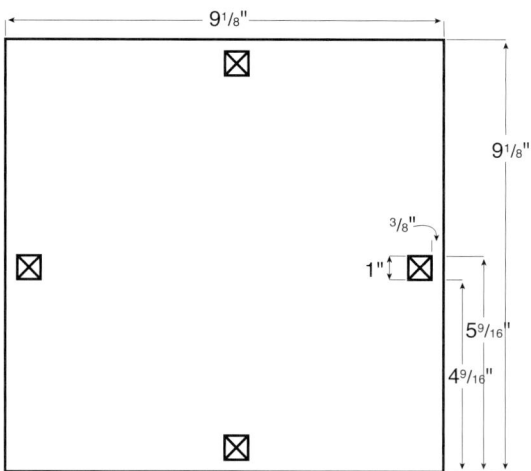

**Fig. 7**
Mark placement of bottom shelf supports on bottom shelf.

and crosspieces from the top with 2-inch screws.

### FINISH

1. Plug all visible screw holes with ⅜-inch walnut plugs, making sure the grain of the plug and the wood run the same direction.

2. Cut the plugs flush with a flush cut saw, or sand flush.

3. Sand table, rounding over all edges.

4. Finish as desired following manufacturer's instructions. ✺

# CHERRY HALL TABLE

Simple joinery creates a sophisticated and intricate look in this table, generously sized to fit a foyer or behind a sofa.

### PROJECT SUPPLIES
44x29x14 inches

### TOOLS
- Miter saw
- Table saw with dado set
- Combination square
- Clamp assortment
- Band saw or jigsaw
- Electric sander (random orbit preferred)
- Drill with 1/8-inch and countersink bits

### SUPPLIES
- 3/4x3/4-inch cherry*: 78 feet
- 1 1/8x1 1/8 cherry*: two 8 foot lengths
- 3/4x14-inch edge-glued cherry panel*: 44 inches
- Sandpaper
- Yellow wood glue
- Clear wood finish
- #8x1 1/2-inch wood or drywall screws
- 3/8-inch flat top wood plugs

*Measurements given are actual, not nominal. Standard nominal lumber will need to be ripped and/or planed to size.

### PROJECT NOTES
This project is built using half-lap joinery cut using a table saw and dado blade. A router and 3/4-inch straight bit may also be used. Be sure to cut some practice pieces before cutting the dados in your work.

### CUTTING
**Lattice**

1. From 3/4x3/4-inch cherry, cut slats as follows: twenty-four 12 1/2-inch lengths (A, B), eight 42 1/2-inch lengths (C) and six 40 1/4-inch lengths (D).

*Note: When cutting dadoes for half laps, cut the same side of the slat each time to ensure proper fitting together of pieces. Slat types are stacked together for cutting.*

2. Set table saw to cut a dado 3/4 inch wide and 3/8 inch deep. *Note: This setting will be used to cut all the slats.*

3. Cut slats as follows, adjusting table saw fence as indicated for each type of slat. *Note: Each time the table saw fence is set, dadoes are to be cut at each end of each slat before the fence is moved, making all the slats of that type identical when the final cut is made.*

**Slats A and B** (twenty-four 12 1/2-inch-long pieces): Set the fence so the first cut begins 1/2-inch from the end of the slat. Make this cut at one end of the slat, then turn the slat 180 degrees, keeping the same side down, and cut the opposite end. Do this with all twenty-four 12 1/2-inch slats. Mark 12 slats to be cut as slat A and the other 12 to be cut as slat B.

**Slat A** (twelve 12 1/2-inch-long pieces): (Fig. 1) Set the table saw fence so the cut begins 3 7/8 inches from the end. Make this cut on both ends of the A slats as before. The 12 A slats now have four dadoes each beginning 1/2 inch and 3 7/8 inches from each side.

**Slat B** (twelve 12 1/2-inch-long pieces): (Fig. 2) Set the table saw fence so the cut begins at 5 7/8 inches. Make one pass with all B slats, cutting a dado in the center of the slat. The 12 B slats

CHERRY HALL TABLE

## ASSEMBLY DIAGRAM

### CHERRY HALL TABLE CUTTING CHART

| P | T | W | L | # |
|---|---|---|---|---|
| A | ¾" | ¾" | 12½" | 12 |
| B | ¾" | ¾" | 12½" | 12 |
| C | ¾" | ¾" | 42½" | 8 |
| D | ¾" | ¾" | 40¼" | 6 |
| E | 1⅛" | 1⅛" | 28¼" | 2 |
| F | 1⅛" | 1⅛" | 28¼" | 2 |
| G | 1⅛" | 1⅛" | 28¼" | 2 |

# CHERRY HALL TABLE

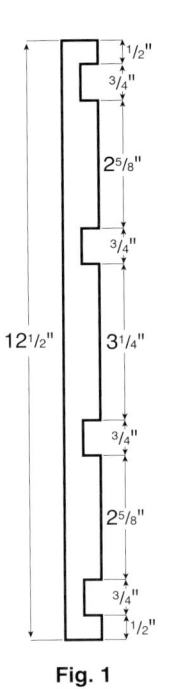

**Fig. 1**
**Slat A**

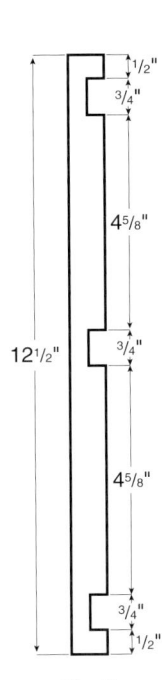

**Fig. 2**
**Slat B**

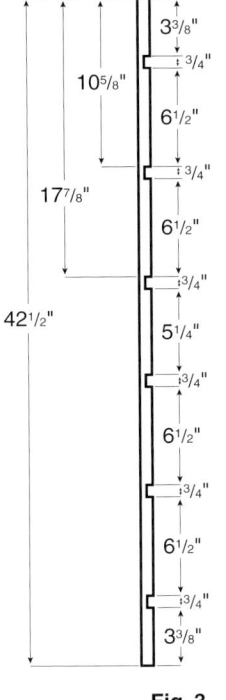

**Fig. 3**
**Slat C**

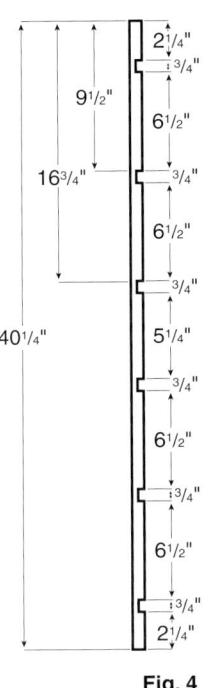

**Fig. 4**
**Slat D**

now have three dadoes each ½ inch from the ends and one in the middle.

**Slat C** (eight 42½-inch-long pieces): (Fig. 3) Set the saw fence so the first set of cuts begins 3⅜ inches from the end of the slat; make two passes, one at each end of each slat. Move the fence so the second set of cuts begins 10⅝ inches in; cut both ends of each slat. Move the fence once more so the last set of cuts begin 17⅞ inches in; cut both ends of each slat.

**Slat D** (six 40¼-inch-long pieces): (Fig. 4) Set the fence so the first set of cuts begins 2¼ inches from the end; cut both ends of each slat. Move the fence so the second set of cuts begins 9½ inches from the end; cut both ends of each slat. Move the fence so the last set of cuts begins 16¾ inches from the end; cut both ends of each slat.

## Legs

**1** From 1⅛x1⅛-inch cherry, cut six 28¼-inch lengths for legs. On each leg, select and mark which side will be out. Four of the legs (corners) will have two sides that will face out; two of the legs (middle) will have only one side that faces out. The inside is that which faces a leg from the opposite side.

**2** Raise the blade of the table saw so it will now make a cut ¾-inch wide by ¾-inch deep.

**3** Referring to Fig. 5, cut each of the six table legs as follows, cutting each leg once before resetting the fence as indicated.

***Notes:*** *Do not cut both ends of the table legs. The first three cuts are measured from the top of the leg and the fourth is measured from the bottom.*

*Make sure each cut in each leg is on the same side (the inside of the leg) as the first cut.*

**First cut**—Set table saw fence so cut begins ¾ inch from the top of the leg.

**Second cut**—Set fence so cut begins 2¼ inches from the top of the leg.

**Third cut**—Set fence so cut begins 3¾ inches from the top of the leg.

**Fourth cut**—Set fence so cut begins 8 inches from the bottom of the table leg.

**4** Separate the four corner legs from the two middle legs; set the middle legs (G) aside.

**5** Separate the four corner legs into two pairs (E, F). Both E legs will be the same and both F legs will be the same. The second pair (F) will be a mirror image of the first pair (E). On both pairs, the corner of the two outside edges of each leg remain straight. The cuts are on the sides facing other legs.

**6** On each of the two (E) legs, draw a line on the bottom of each leg ½ inch from the outside edge; extend that line onto the side of the leg. On the side that will face other legs, draw a line from the bottom of the bottom dado to the extended ½-inch mark (Fig. 6). Cut the taper using a band saw or jigsaw. Repeat on the second side of the same leg. Sand smooth.

**7** Cut tapers on each of the two (F) legs in the same manner so that, when assembled, (F) legs mirror the (E) legs (Fig. 7).

**8** On each of the two middle legs (G), measure in from the outside ½ inch on the bottom of the leg; extend this line up the sides. Draw a line from the bottom of the bottom dado to the extended ½-inch marks. This will be the taper for the back of the leg.

**9** Measuring in again from the side of the leg (on the bottom) and mark the center; measure back out ¼ inch toward each side and extend these lines up the front. Draw a line across from the bottom of the bottom dado to the front of the leg on each side. On each of the two middle legs (G), measure in from the sides ¼ inch and mark on the bottom of the leg. Extend the marks to the front and back of the leg so you can see them. Draw a line from the bottom of the bottom dado to the extended

lines at the bottom of the fronts and backs of the legs. The end result is a leg that is tapered on both sides and the back, but the face is straight, albeit narrower at the bottom (Fig. 8). Cut tapers with a band saw or jigsaw; sand smooth.

### ASSEMBLE & FINISH
#### Lattice & legs

**1** Hand-sand slats, being sure not to alter any of the half-laps, and avoiding the last 1⅛ inches of each end of the C slats as this is the part that will fit into the legs.

**2** Referring to Fig. 9, dry-fit slats together as follows to create four lattices: Use two C slats as outside runners on each lattice. Complete two lattices with one D slat in the middle and B slats crossing them (lattice B). Complete the remaining

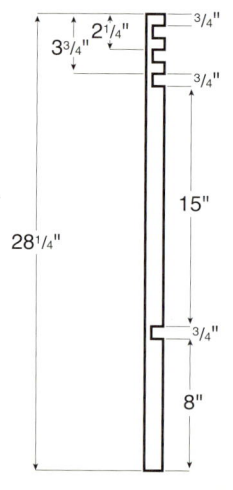

**Fig. 5**
Cut dadoes in all six legs.

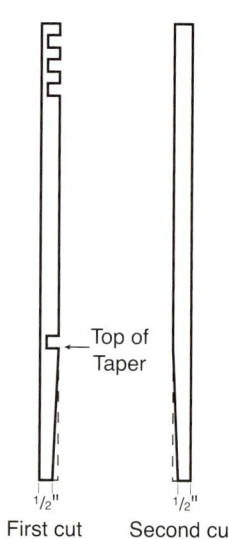

**Fig. 6**
Cut tapers on corner (E) legs.

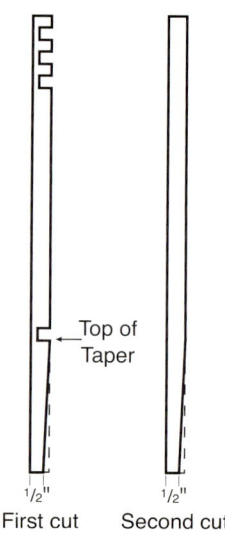

**Fig. 7**
Cut tapers on corner (F) legs.

**Fig. 8**
Cut tapers on (G) legs.

# CHERRY HALL TABLE

two lattices with two D slats in the middle and A slats as cross pieces (lattice A).

**3** Find the center of each Slat C and mark the outside edge. Move toward each end 9/16 inch and make a mark. Draw a line across this mark. This is where the center leg will receive the slat.

**4** Separate each lattice, then apply a slight amount of glue in each half-lap; reassemble and clamp together. Remove excess glue and let dry.

**5** Use tape to mask off 1⅛ inches at each end of the A slats and at the middle of each runner (marked in step 2). Apply clear wood finish per manufacturer's instructions. Let dry; remove tape.

**6** Apply clear wood finish to legs, taking care not to get finish in the dadoes.

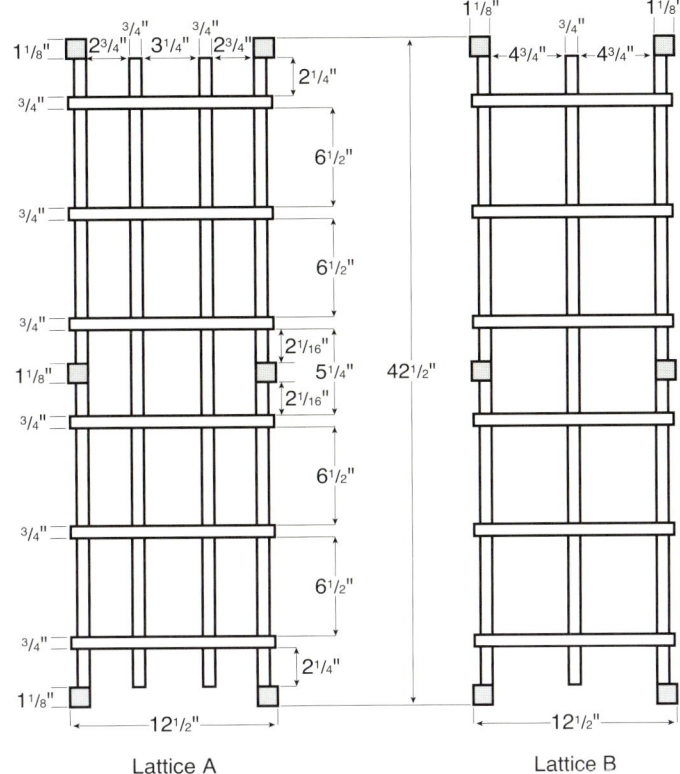

**Fig. 9**
Lattice Assembly

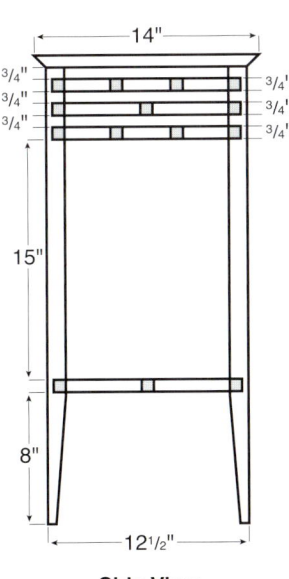

**Side View**

CHERRY HALL TABLE

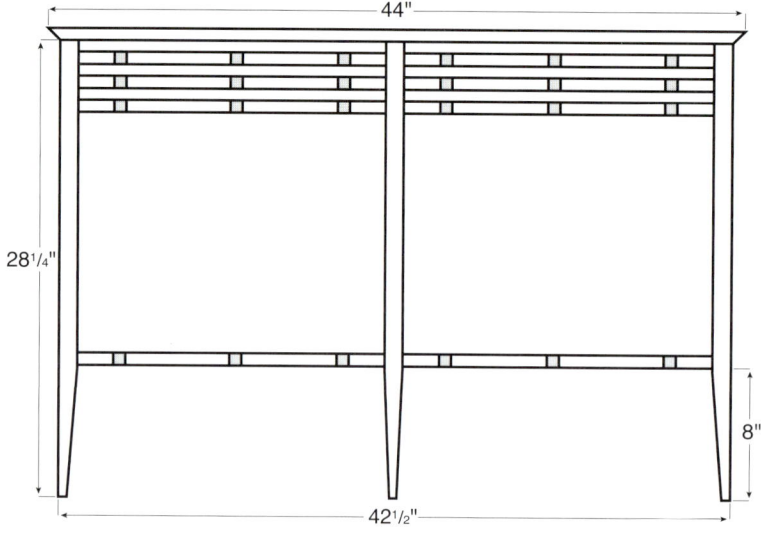

**Front View**

**7** Place legs E, F and G on a flat surface with dadoes up. Using just a slight amount of glue in the dadoes, glue the two A lattices into the top and third leg dadoes. The outside of the corner legs should be flush with the end of the lattice shelf, and the middle leg at the center marks. Clamp each joint and let dry.

**8** Glue the two B lattices into the second and bottom dadoes. Clamp in place and let dry.

9. Leaving the table in the same position, glue and clamp remaining legs E, F and G in place; let dry.

## Tabletop

1. Referring to Fig. 10, draw a line on the underside of the tabletop ¾ inch from the edge around the perimeter. Place the assembled table base onto the upside down tabletop; mark placement of the six table legs.

2. Remove the table base and stand it up. Draw an X in each square where the table legs were. Drill a hole completely through the tabletop at the center of the X (Fig. 11).

3. Turn the tabletop upright and clamp the tabletop to the base where it belongs; drill and countersink a hole at the pilot holes and into the top of each leg.

4. Unclamp and remove tabletop. Cut the ¾-inch bevel on the tabletop using the table saw. Sand the underside of the tabletop and apply clear wood finish; let dry.

5. Attach the tabletop to the base with 1½-inch screws. Glue in wood plugs; matching grain with the tabletop; let dry.

6. Trim off wood plugs and sand tabletop. Apply clear wood finish to top of tabletop according to manufacturer's instructions; let dry.

7. Using 220-grit sandpaper, lightly hand-sand assembled table and apply a second coat of clear wood finish to entire piece.

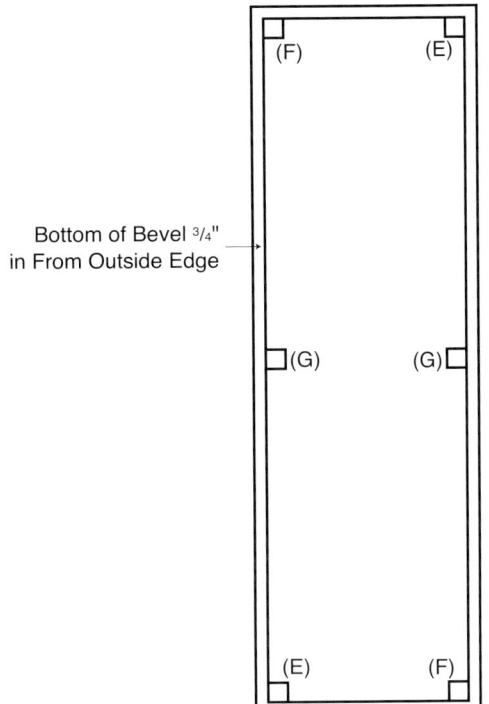

**Fig. 10**
**Bottom View of Tabletop**

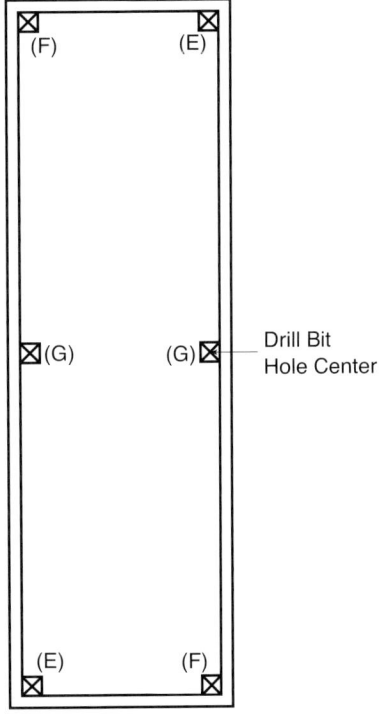

**Fig. 11**
**Top View of Tabletop**

# CIRCULAR COFFEE TABLE

A circle cutting jig makes this project easy, and the exposed wood plies create a striking layered effect.

**PROJECT SUPPLIES**
23¾x13¾ inches

**TOOLS**
- Combination square
- Drill with ⅛-inch, ⅜-inch and 15⁄16-inch brad point bits, 1-inch Forstner bit and #8 countersink with drill bit
- Jasper circle cutting jig
- Router with plunge capacity, with ¼-inch spiral upcut router bit and ½x2-inch long flush trim bit
- Table saw
- Miter saw
- Band saw or jigsaw
- Sander
- Socket wrench or ratchet with ⅜-inch socket

**SUPPLIES**
- ¾-inch birch veneer plywood: four 24-inch squares
- ⅜x24x24-inch backer board material
- ¾x8-inch mahogany*: 8 inches
- 4x4-inch mahogany*: 48 inches
- Double-sided tape
- Eight #8x2-inch wood or drywall screws
- Four ⅜x3½-inch lag bolts
- Four ⅜x1-inch washers
- One 1-inch wood screw
- One ⅜-inch birch wood plug
- Clear wood finish

*Measurements given are actual, not nominal. Standard nominal lumber will need to be ripped and/or planed to size.

*Note:* A dust mask is essential when working with woods such as mahogany and walnut as the sawdust from such woods is toxic and can do serious and long-term damage to your lungs.

## CUTTING

*Notes: Each of the four 24-inch-square pieces of birch veneer plywood will be cut to a 23¾-inch-diameter circle. A 7-inch-diameter circle will be cut from the top piece (A), and a 15-inch-diameter circle will be cut from each of the bottom two pieces (C, D).*

*Check with the manufacturer's directions for their recommendation on how deep your router can make each cut. Reset the depth after each pass until you cut all the way through the ¾-inch thickness. Depending on the router, it may take five or six passes to cut all the way through the plywood.*

**Top piece**

1. Place backer board on workbench. Place several strips of double-sided tape on the backer board within a 1-foot radius from the center. Determine which of the four ¾-inch birch veneer plywood pieces will be the top of the table; place that piece on the backer board.

2. Using the combination square to make sure the corners are square, draw a line from one corner to its diagonal opposite, then do the same with the other two corners. Drill a ⅛-inch hole at the center of the X deep enough to go through the ¾-inch plywood, but not all the way through the backer board.

3. Set the pin from the circle cutting jig into the hole securely. Make sure it is set all the way in by tapping the pin with a hammer. Mount your router to the jig, then mount the jig onto the pin following the manufacturer's instructions.

4. With the jig set at the 23½-inch index hole, and the router base and jig sitting flat on the plywood, turn the router on and plunge it into

CIRCULAR COFFEE TABLE

# ASSEMBLY DIAGRAM

| P | T | W | L | # |
|---|---|---|---|---|
| **CIRCULAR COFFEE TABLE CUTTING CHART** | | | | |
| A | ¾" | 23¾" in diameter | | 1 |
| B | ¾" | 23¾" in diameter | | 1 |
| C | ¾" | 23¾" in diameter | | 1 |
| D | ¾" | 23¾" in diameter | | 1 |
| E | ¾" | 7½" in diameter | | 1 |
| F | 3" | 3" | 11" | 4 |

the plywood. Cut a path through the top, resetting the depth of the cut each time.

5. Reset the jig at the 7-inch index hole. Make passes around the circle, resetting the depth until this is cut out. Remove top piece (A) from backer board.

### Second piece

Place second piece on the backer board. Repeat steps 2–4 of tabletop. Remove second piece (B) from backer board.

### Third & fourth pieces

1. Place piece C on the backer board. Repeat steps 2–4 of tabletop.

2. Reset the jig at the 15-inch index hole. Make passes around the circle resetting the depth until this is cut out. Remove the piece (C) from the backer board.

3. Duplicate steps 1 and 2 for piece D so that C and D are identical.

### Table insert

1. Find the center of the 8x8-inch mahogany as in step 2 of tabletop; drill a 1/8-inch hole.

2. Install the circle cutting jig set at the 7½-inch index hole; cut the insert (E).

3. Trial-fit the insert (E) into the top piece (A) and adjust to fit, if necessary, with light sanding on the edges.

4. Once the insert fits, sand the top, rounding the edges slightly.

### Table legs

1. Using the table saw, rip the 4x4-inch mahogany to 3x3 inches square.

2. Using the miter saw, cut four 11-inch lengths from the 3x3-inch mahogany (ripped in step 1) for the legs (F). **Note:** *Cut on the waste side of the line.* Determine which end will be the top and the bottom of each leg.

3. Mark the center width of each leg side, extending the line the entire length of the leg on each side and across the top and the bottom. **Note:** *This will create an X on the top and the bottom of each leg.* Measure 5¼-inches from the top of each leg and draw a horizontal line all the way around each leg.

4. Cut out or copy the leg template. Lay it in place on the table leg and temporarily secure with tape. Mark the cut lines. Do this on all four sides of each leg.

5. With the 5/16-inch brad point drill bit, drill a hole 2½ inches deep in the top of each leg at the center of the X. Set the table legs aside to finish cutting prior to assembly.

### ASSEMBLE & FINISH

1. Extend the centering lines on the four tabletop and frame pieces (A, B, C and D) down the outside

## CIRCULAR COFFEE TABLE

edges; extend the lines down the inside edges of the three circle cutouts (A, C and D). With top side of piece A exposed, glue and clamp pieces A and B together, matching edge lines. Glue and clamp pieces C and D with unmarked sides together, matching edge lines. Let dry.

**2** Turn the legs (F) upside down so the top of each leg rests on the table bottom (C/D). Determine which corner of each leg will face out and match that corner of each leg to each of the outside edge lines. Match the back corner to the inside lines and trace around the legs. Remove the legs and draw lines from corner to corner in the square outline of each leg. With the 1/8-inch brad point drill bit, drill pilot holes through piece C/D at the center of each X. Turn piece C/D over. Using the 1-inch Forstner bit, drill a hole 5/8 inch deep at each 1/8-inch pilot hole. Redrill each pilot hole using a 3/8-inch brad point bit.

**3** With the band saw or jigsaw, cut legs according to the template marks made earlier. Sand smooth.

**4** Turn the tabletop (A/B) face down; place the frame (C/D) on it, matching edge marks. Make sure the 1-inch holes are sandwiched and the leg placement marks are visible. Screw these units together with six to eight of the 2-inch screws, drilled and countersunk. Trim the edges of the tabletop with the flush trim router bit. This will take several passes. Sand the edges of the table smooth.

**5** Separate the tabletop (A/B) from the frame (C/D). Using the 3/8x3 1/2-inch lags and washers, attach the legs to the table frame. Tighten with the socket wrench. Reattach the tabletop and frame with the 2-inch wood screws. There is no need to glue these sections together.

**6** Predrill a 3/8-inch hole 3/8 inch deep in the center of the mahogany insert. Be sure the tabletop cutout and the mahogany insert are free from dust and debris. Glue the underside of the insert into the cutout. Secure with one 1-inch wood screw.

**7** Glue the 3/8-inch birch plug in place and trim flush. Sand tabletop; remove all dust.

**8** Finish entire table with clear coat following manufacturer's instructions. ✻

CIRCULAR COFFEE TABLE

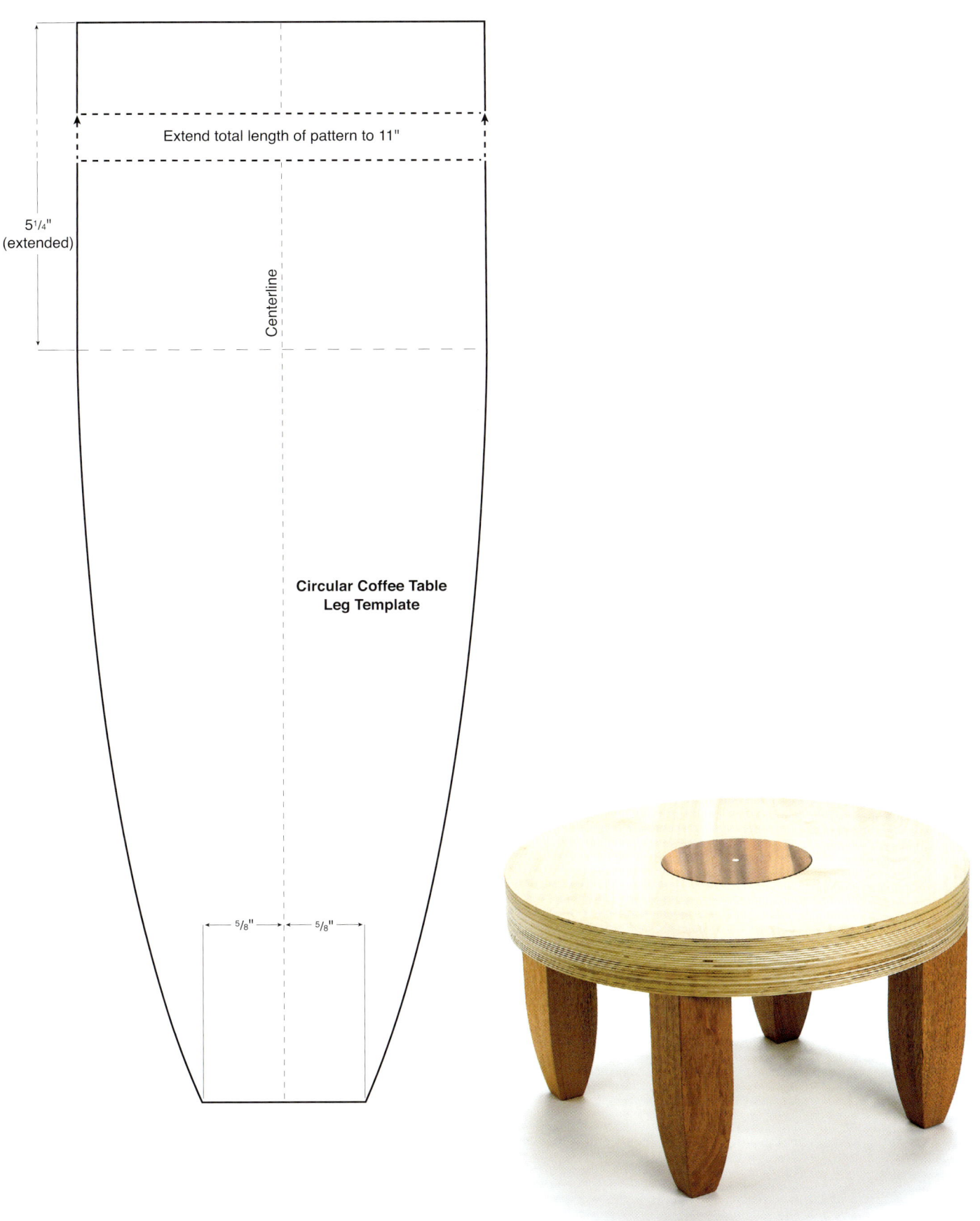

Extend total length of pattern to 11"

5 1/4" (extended)

Centerline

**Circular Coffee Table
Leg Template**

5/8"  5/8"

# GEOMETRIC ILLUSIONS TABLE

**PROJECT SIZE**
34½x13¾x33 inches

**TOOLS**
- Table saw with regular and 8-inch dado blade sets
- Flush-cut saw
- Dowel-It self-centering dowel jig
- Drill with 1/16- and ¼-inch brad-point bits and ¾-inch Forstner bit
- Combination square
- Assorted clamps

**SUPPLIES**
- ¾x9¼-inch jatoba*: 6 feet (or six one-foot lengths; board may also be as narrow as 8½ inches)
- ¾-inch plywood: 16x30 inches (for jigs)
- 1/8x¾-inch walnut *: 96 inches (minimum of one 12-inch and six 13-inch lengths)
- 1½x3½-inch walnut*: 8 feet
- 1½x2½-inch walnut*: 6 feet
- 1½x1½-inch walnut*: 3 feet
- 1¼-inch screws (for jigs)
- Cyanoacrylate glue
- Fifteen to twenty ¾x1½-inch dowels
- Miller dowels and stepped drill bit size 1X: 16 walnut
- Wood glue
- Sandpaper: medium- to fine-grit
- Danish oil
- Four figure-eight fasteners

*Measurements given are actual, not nominal. Standard nominal lumber will need to be ripped and/or planed to size.

## Sleek and sculptural, this pedestal table makes a bold statement.

*Note: A dust mask is essential when working with woods such as mahogany and walnut as the sawdust from such woods is toxic and can do serious and long-term damage to your lungs.*

### TABLETOP
**Cutting jatoba**

**1** From jatoba, cut one 24-inch length. Rip this piece to 8½ inches wide, then cut into two 10¼-inch lengths for tabletop pieces (B). **Option:** Rip two 1-foot lengths to 8½ inches; crosscut into two 10¼-inch lengths.

**2** Rip the remaining 4-foot piece to 8 inches wide, then cut into four 11-inch lengths for tabletop middle pieces (A). *Note: The six pieces of jatoba from steps 1 and 2 are the primary tabletop pieces.*

**3** On the bottom edge of each A piece, measure and mark 2 inches from one side; carry the line over the edge to mark the end grain. In the same manner, mark both B pieces 1¾ inches in from one side (Fig 1).

**4** Rip the ¾-inch plywood into one 9x30-inch piece and one 7x30-inch piece. Set the 7-inch piece aside for the pedestal jig.

**5** Cut the 9-inch piece to 20 inches long for the jig base. From the remaining 10-inch length, rip two 2-inch-wide pieces; cut each of the 2x10-inch pieces in half to make four 2x5-inch pieces for the jig fence.

**6** Place the first 8-inch piece of jatoba on the jig base so the top corner and the 2-inch mark at the bottom is even with the edge of the jig (Fig. 2). *Note: The part resting on the jig base is the tabletop piece; the part hanging over is waste.* Place one of the 2x5-inch fence pieces tight against the back edge of the 8-inch piece, check to be sure the tabletop piece is where it should be, and fasten fence into the base with two 1¼-inch screws. Fasten another fence piece at the top and a third piece at the bottom to hold the tabletop piece in place.

**7** Set the table saw fence so the jig base fits exactly between the blade and the fence; set the blade height at 1½ inches. Cut all four A jatoba pieces using the jig.

GEOMETRIC ILLUSIONS TABLE

## ASSEMBLY DIAGRAM

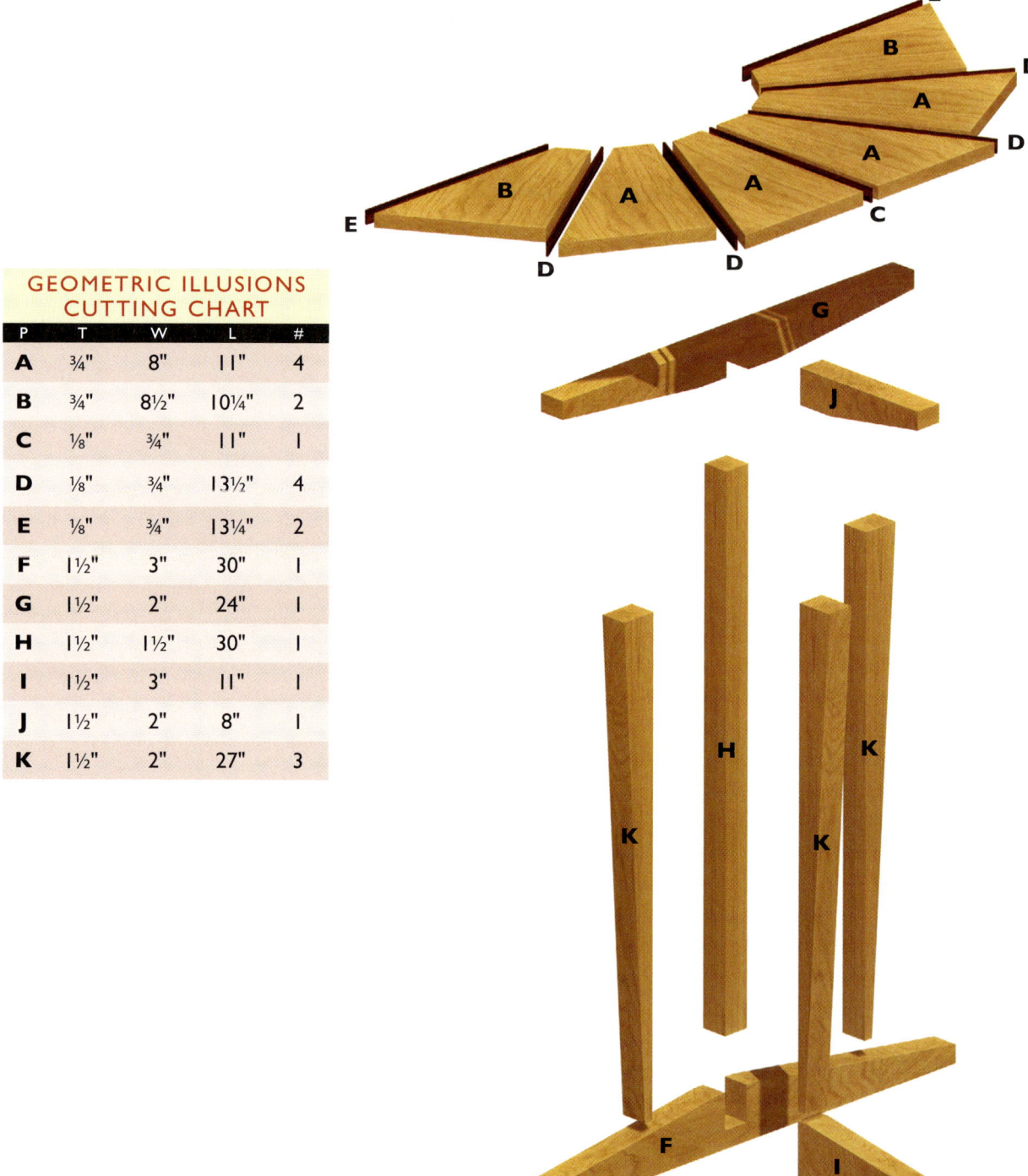

| GEOMETRIC ILLUSIONS CUTTING CHART | | | | |
|---|---|---|---|---|
| P | T | W | L | # |
| A | ¾" | 8" | 11" | 4 |
| B | ¾" | 8½" | 10¼" | 2 |
| C | ⅛" | ¾" | 11" | 1 |
| D | ⅛" | ¾" | 13½" | 4 |
| E | ⅛" | ¾" | 13¼" | 2 |
| F | 1½" | 3" | 30" | 1 |
| G | 1½" | 2" | 24" | 1 |
| H | 1½" | 1½" | 30" | 1 |
| I | 1½" | 3" | 11" | 1 |
| J | 1½" | 2" | 8" | 1 |
| K | 1½" | 2" | 27" | 3 |

# GEOMETRIC ILLUSIONS TABLE

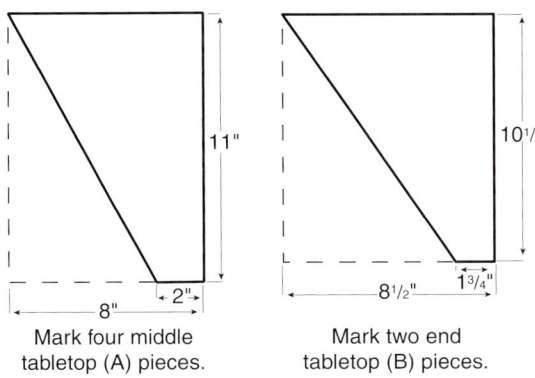

Fig. 1
Layout for
Jatoba Tabletop Pieces

Mark four middle tabletop (A) pieces.

Mark two end tabletop (B) pieces.

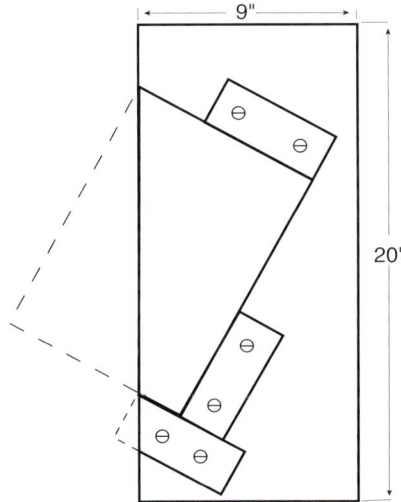

Fig. 2
Secure tabletop piece on plywood base of jig using 2"x5" fence pieces.

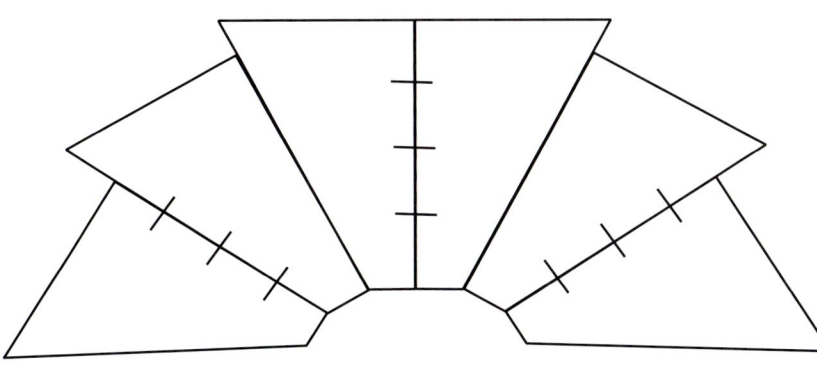

Fig. 3
Dowel Placement

**8** Remove the fences from the jig. Place one of the two B tabletop pieces on the jig base and attach fences as in step 6. Cut both B tabletop pieces as in step 7.

## Walnut accent

**1** From ⅛x¾-inch walnut strip, cut one 11-inch (C), four 13½-inch (D) and two 13¼-inch lengths for tabletop accent pieces (E).

**2** Using the cyanoacrylate glue, attach one walnut accent piece (D and E) to the long angle side of each jatoba piece (A and B) and the 11-inch piece (C) to one 11-inch edge of one of the 8x11-inch pieces (A). Let dry; trim with flush-cut saw.

## TABLETOP ASSEMBLE & FINISH

**1** Referring to Fig. 3, lay out tabletop pieces (A, B) with the four A pieces in the middle and the B pieces on the ends. Mark three or four lines on each adjoining pair for dowel placement. Using the dowel centering jig, drill ¾-inch deep holes in each piece at each mark, then dowel, glue and clamp each table top pair together. ***Note:*** *Use the waste angle pieces for a better clamping grip.* Let dry.

**2** Lay out pieces in their final positions. Mark dowel locations on the two remaining joints; drill holes and join as above. Let dry.

**3** Sand tabletop progressively, beginning with medium-grit and finishing with fine-grit sandpaper. Remove dust.

GEOMETRIC ILLUSIONS TABLE

**Fig. 4**
Cut 1½x1" dado in long top support piece.

4 Following manufacturer's instruction, apply three coats of Danish oil. Set aside.

### BASE
*Note: The table base consists of the tabletop support (two pieces), the pedestal (three identical pieces and one pedestal post) and the foot (two pieces).*

**Cutting length**

1 From the 8-foot walnut, cut a 43-inch length. Rip this length to 3 inches wide, then cut one 30-inch length (F) and one 11-inch length (I) for the foot pieces. Rip the remaining 53-inch length to 2 inches wide, then cut one 27-inch length for one of the pedestal pieces (K) and one 24-inch length for long tabletop support (G).

2 Rip the 6-foot walnut to 2 inches wide, then cut two more 27-inch long pedestal pieces (K) and one 8-inch length for short table top support (J).

3 From the 3-foot walnut, cut a 30-inch length for the pedestal post (H).

**Cutting dadoes**

1 Using the complete dado set in the table saw to get as wide a cut as possible, set the blade height to 1 inch. *Note: Refer to Fig. 4 to lay out the position of the dado in the long top support piece.* On the 24-inch top support piece (G), mark a line across the 1½-inch width 1 inch down each side and 11¼ inches from each end. Place the pedestal post (H) between these lines to make sure the width is correct.

2 Line up the marks so the blade will cut between the marks. Set

# GEOMETRIC ILLUSIONS TABLE

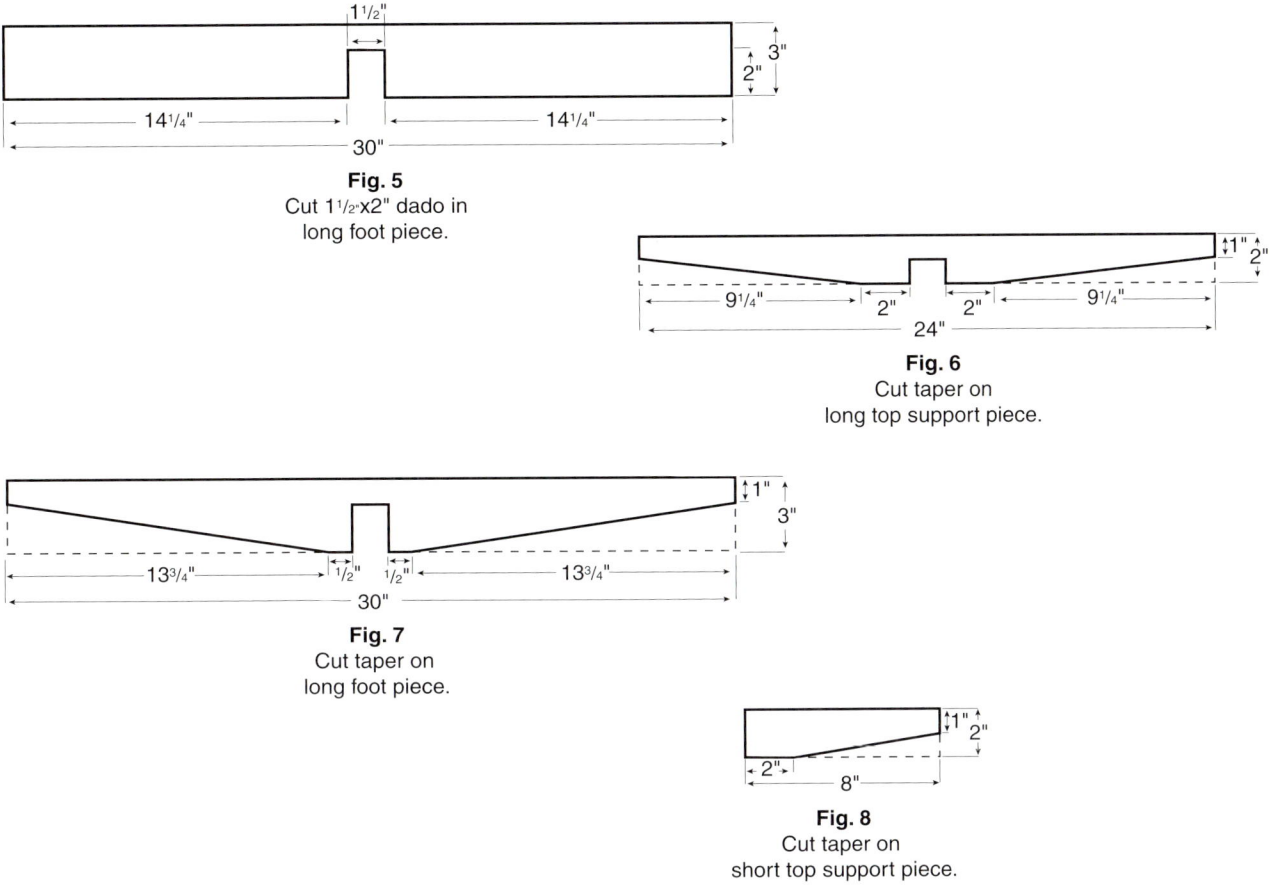

**Fig. 5** Cut 1½"x2" dado in long foot piece.

**Fig. 6** Cut taper on long top support piece.

**Fig. 7** Cut taper on long foot piece.

**Fig. 8** Cut taper on short top support piece.

the stop on the table-saw miter gauge at the end of the top support. Make the first pass, flip the piece side to side and make the second cut. Test-fit the pedestal post.

3. Raise the dado blade height to 2 inches. **Note:** *Refer to Fig. 5 to lay out the dado in the long foot piece.* On the 30-inch foot piece (F), mark a line across the 1½-inch width and down the sides 14¼ inches from each end. Place the pedestal post between these lines to make sure the width is correct.

4. Line up the marks so the blade will cut between the marks. Set the stop on the table saw miter gauge at the end of the top support. Make the first pass, flip the piece side to side and make the second cut. Test fit the pedestal post.

## Cutting angles

1. Change the table-saw blade back to the straight blade. Set the blade height slightly higher than 2¼ inches. Adjust the jig that was made to cut the tabletop pieces to cut an angle on the 24-inch top support piece (G) from 9¼ inches in from the end to 1 inch at the end. Set the fences and cut each end (Fig. 6).

2. Move the fences to cut an angle on the 30-inch foot piece (F) ends from 13¾ inches in from the end to 1 inch at the end. Cut each end (Fig. 7) Move the fences to cut an angle on the 8-inch top support piece (J); double check settings, then cut piece (Fig. 8). Move the fences again to cut the 11-inch foot piece; double check settings, then cut piece (Fig. 9).

3. Sand out all saw marks, beginning with medium-grit and progressing to fine-grit sandpaper, taking care to not round over corners.

4. Using the 7x30-inch plywood base cut earlier and several 2x5 inch fence pieces (reuse first set or rip more), prepare to build the pedestal jig for the base pieces. Set the table-saw fence to the width of the

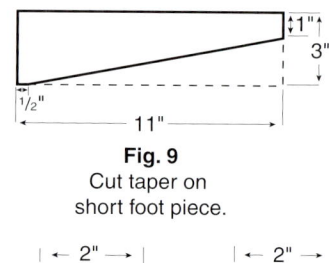

**Fig. 9**
Cut taper on short foot piece.

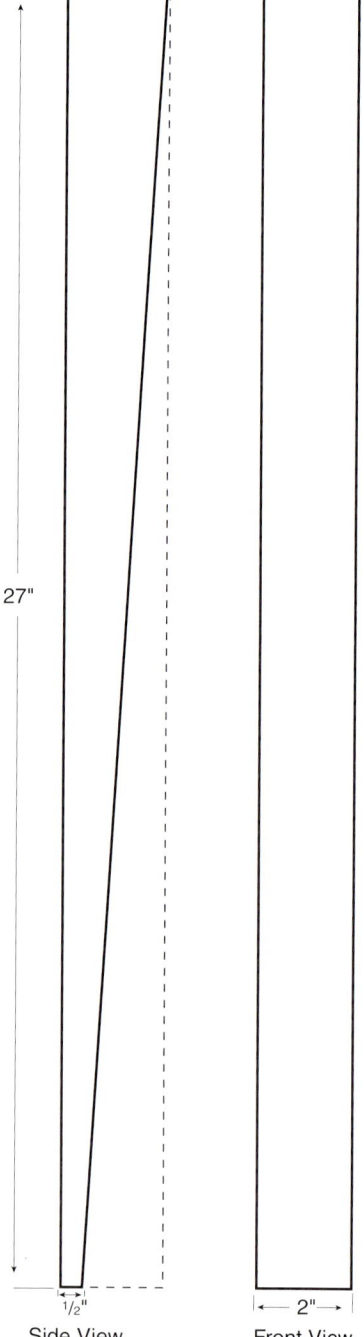

**Fig. 10**
Cut taper on pedestal piece.

plywood base and the blade height to 2¾ inches.

5 Mark the bottom of one of the pedestal pieces (K) ½ inch from the back toward the front. This piece will be 1½x2 inches at the top and 1½x½ inch at the bottom (Fig. 10). With the wide end to the front of the jig, place the first piece on the jig base so the top corner and the ½-inch mark at the bottom are even with the edge of the jig. **Note:** *The part resting on the jig base is the pedestal piece; the part hanging over is waste.*

6 Place one of the 2x5-inch fence pieces tight against the back edge of one K piece; check to be sure it is where it should be, and fasten the fence into the base with two 1¼-inch screws. Fasten another fence piece at the top and one more at the bottom to hold the pedestal piece in place. Cut all three K pedestal pieces using the jig. **Note:** *Make sure the piece does not lift from the jig. Keep fingers and hands clear of the blade.*

7 Sand out all saw marks, except for the pedestal post (H), beginning with medium-grit and progressing to fine-grit sandpaper, taking care to not round over corners.

### BASE ASSEMBLE & FINISH

*Note: Join the table base pieces together using the Miller dowel system. Follow the package directions for the step down bit and dowels.*

1 Mark the bottom of the 3x30-inch foot piece (F) for dowel placement with two lines toward the center ⅜ inch in from the edge and two lines toward the center ⅜ inch in from the edge of the dado (Fig. 11). **Note:** *Dowel locations will be right under the dado.* Brush glue onto the sides and bottom of the dado and set the pedestal post in the dado. Clamp together.

2 Drill the first dowel hole; glue and tap the ribbed dowel into place, then repeat for the other three holes. Cut dowel ends off with a flush-cut saw. Repeat to attach the top support piece (G) to the pedestal post.

3 Glue and clamp one of the pedestal pieces (K) to each side of the pedestal post (H) with the 2-inch end at the top. Let dry, then sand off excess glue.

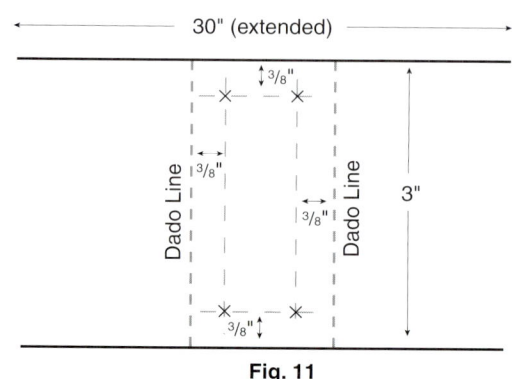

**Fig. 11**
Mark bottom of 30" foot piece for dowel placement.

# GEOMETRIC ILLUSIONS TABLE

**4** Mark dowel locations on the bottom back of the foot piece (F) and the pedestal post for attaching the J foot piece. Beginning at the bottom of the foot piece and centered on the post (H), mark every ⅜ inch until four locations are marked (Fig. 12).

**5** Apply glue to the back of the foot piece (I) and clamp in place; drill one hole, glue and tap in a dowel. Repeat until all four dowels are in place. Trim the ends off with the flush-cut saw.

**6** Glue and clamp the remaining pedestal piece (K) in place on the front above foot piece (I).

**7** Glue and set the 8-inch top support (J), angle down, on top of the pedestal piece and against the other top support and post. Clamp in place. Mark drill locations in the top of this 8-inch top support; glue and tap four dowels in place, then cut off ends with flush-cut saw. Sand off excess glue.

**8** Sand progressively, beginning with medium-grit and finishing with fine-grit sandpaper. Remove dust.

**9** Apply three coats of Danish oil following manufacturer's instructions.

## FINAL ASSEMBLY

**1** Drill one ¾-inch hole ⅛ inch deep 6 inches from each end of the top support (G) and ½ inch from the back edge.

**2** Drill two ¾-inch holes ⅛ inch deep in the 8-inch top support piece (J): one 3 inches out from the back and ½ inch in from the left side; the other 4½ inches out from the back and ½ inch in from the right side.

**3** Attach the four figure-eight fasteners in these holes.

**4** Set the tabletop on the frame with the back inset edge of the top flush with the back of the frame, and the back sides evenly spaced away from the frame (2¾ inches). Mark fastener locations on the bottom of the table. Drill pilot holes, then secure the top to the frame with the screws provided with the fasteners. ✺

**Back View of Assembled Top Support, Pedestal & Foot**

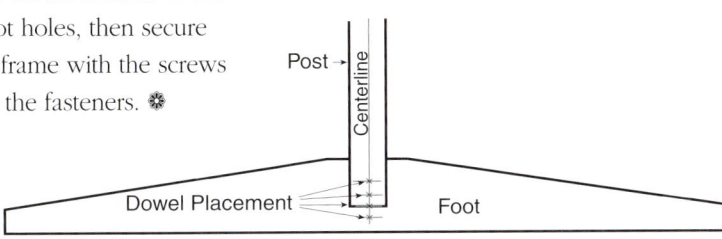

**Fig. 12**
Mark placement of dowels for attaching 11" foot.

# WALNUT & WENGE COFFEE TABLE

Experiment with exotic woods for an elegant and up-to-the-minute look.

### PROJECT SIZE
44⅞x24⅜x16¼ inches

### TOOLS
- Plunge router with ¼-inch spiral bit and template guide, or jigsaw
- Disc sander with assortment of disc grits
- Flexible curve
- Table saw with regular blade and 8-inch dado blade set (or optional ¾-inch straight router bit and edge guide)
- 48-inch straight edge
- Shaping tool (Sur-form pocket plane, rasps, files, spoke shave or other)
- Assorted clamps
- Combination square
- Drill with ¾-inch Forstner bit, and 1/16-inch straight bit

### SUPPLIES
- ¾x25-inch Peruvian walnut*: two 45-inch lengths
- ¼-inch Baltic birch plywood: one 12½x45-inch piece and one 12x22-inch piece (for templates)
- ¾x3½-inch Peruvian walnut*: two 14-inch lengths (for end uprights) and one 25-inch length (for middle upright)
- 1¾x3½-inch wenge**: four 19½-inch lengths (for legs)
- 1¾x1¾-inch wenge**: two 26-inch lengths (for cross supports)
- ¾x7x30-inch scrap plywood (for taper jig base)
- Four ¾x2x5-inch plywood pieces (for jig fences)
- Wood glue
- Masking tape
- Eight 1¼-inch screws
- Clear finish
- Eight figure-eight fasteners

*If not available for purchase in this size, glue up enough Peruvian walnut boards to make two ¾x25x45-inch panels (with the grain running with the 45-inch length), and one ¾x25x12-inch panel (with the grain running the 12-inch length).

**Measurements given are actual, not nominal. Standard nominal lumber will need to be ripped and/or planed to size.

**Note:** *A dust mask is essential when working with woods such as mahogany and walnut as the sawdust from such woods is toxic and can do serious and long term damage to your lungs.*

### PREPARATION

**1** Determine which of the ¾x25x45-inch panels (A) will be top and bottom; mark them accordingly. Draw a line down the center lengthwise on each piece, extending over the edges at both ends. For dado locations, measure and mark along the long edges at ¾ and 22⅛ inches in from each end; draw the lines across the width of the panel connecting these marks (Fig. 1).

**2** Using the ¼x12½x45-inch plywood to create the tabletop panel template, draw a center line the width of the board. Referring to the Tabletop Panel Template, mark all dimensions. With the flexible curve, draw a curved line beginning from the top of the center line, down through the 5¾-inch mark and connecting to the 7-inch mark on the end of the plywood.

WALNUT & WENGE COFFEE TABLE

## ASSEMBLY DIAGRAM

| P | T | W | L | # |
|---|---|---|---|---|
| **WALNUT & WENGE CUTTING CHART** | | | | |
| A | ¾" | 25" | 45" | 2 |
| B | ¾" | 25" | 3½" | 1 |
| C | ¾" | 14" | 3½" | 2 |
| D | 1¾" | 3½" | 19½" | 4 |
| E | 1¾" | 1¾" | 26" | 2 |

# WALNUT & WENGE COFFEE TABLE

**3** Using the ¼x12x22-inch plywood to create the end arc template, draw a center line the width of the board. Referring to the end arc template drawing, mark all dimensions. With the center of the flexible curve on the center line, and the ends at each 1¼x7⅝-inch mark, draw the curved line, extending line slightly past the 7⅝ inch marks.

**4** Cutting slightly to the waste side of the arc lines, cut each template with the plunge router and ¼-inch spiral bit or with the jigsaw. Use the disc sander with an 80- or 100-grit sanding disc to sand off waste to the lines.

## TABLETOP

*Note: Use either the dado set and table saw (if the table-saw deck will support a 45-inch panel) or the router and ¾-inch straight bit with the edge guide, to cut the two rabbets and the dado in the bottom of the top panel (A) and the top of the bottom panel (A).*

**1** Place the tabletop panel template on the bottom panel (A), matching center lines; clamp in place, making sure there is sufficient clearance for the router. With the template guide set and securely in the router, rout the curve, plunging no more than ¼ inch at a time. Make several passes to cut through the ¾-inch panel. Repeat for the opposite long side of the bottom panel and both long sides of the top panel.

**2** Place the end arc template on the end of one panel (A), making sure the template center line matches the panel center line. Clamp in place and cut as above. Repeat for the opposite end of the same panel and both ends of the remaining panel.

**3** Clamp top and bottom panels (A) together so all edges are flush. Sand with disc sander and medium-grit sanding disc until the cut lines are gone and the two panels are identical.

**4** Unclamp the pieces. Using a 220-grit disc, sand the underside of the top panel, both sides of the bottom panel, both sides of the ¾x25x3½-inch middle upright (B) (taking care not to sand too close to the long edges) and the inside face of both ¾x25x14-inch end uprights (C).

**5** Dry fit the middle upright (B) in the top and bottom panels. Trace the outline of the table ends onto the top and bottom of the end uprights (C). Remove one end upright; cut it to match the tabletop using the band saw, then shape the outside edge using the shaping tool. Repeat for other end upright.

**6** Tape-off all finish areas where glue squeeze-out could occur. Glue and clamp together tabletops (A and A) and uprights (B and C); let glue cure.

**7** Remove clamps. Sand table top and bottom, and the outside face of the end uprights. Set assembled unit aside.

## LEG FRAME

*Note: The joint used to attach the legs to the cross supports is called a*

**Fig. 1**
**Tabletop Dado Placement**
Dados are cut in bottom of top panel and in top of bottom panel.

## WALNUT & WENGE COFFEE TABLE

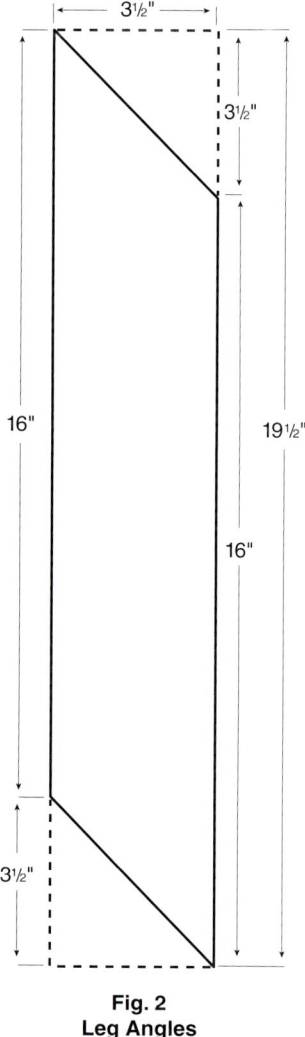

**Fig. 2**
**Leg Angles**

bridle joint. It consists of an open mortise at the top end of each leg and a through tenon on both ends of each cross support.

1. With the miter gauge set to cut a 45-degree angle and the straight blade in the table saw, make parallel cuts on the ends of each table leg (D) so the overall length of each leg is 19½ inches (Fig. 2).

2. Cut each end of each cross support (E) to a 45-degree angle so the long-point measurement is 26 inches and the cuts go toward each other (Fig. 3).

3. To cut the open mortises in the top of each leg (D), set the dado blade cut width to ⅝ inch. Set the table-saw fence so the dado blade cuts through the center of the top of the leg. **Note:** *Use a tall fence and clamps, or make a jig attached to the table saw fence (Fig. 4), to hold the top of the leg flat to the table-saw deck.* Begin cutting the first leg with the blade only ½ inch high and make several passes, raising the blade after each pass until the full 1¾ inches is cut. **Note:** *Use one of the cross pieces as a height indicator for the blade. Repeat to cut an open mortise in each of the remaining three legs (Fig. 5).*

4. To cut tenons in the cross supports (E), set the miter gauge to a 45-degree angle, the dado blade as wide as possible and the height to 9/16 inch. At the top and bottom of a cross support, mark 5 inches in from each end and draw a line to connect the marks. **Note:** *This should yield a 45-degree line parallel to the end, with the measurement between marks on the top being 12½ inches and on the bottom being 16 inches.* Set the stop on the miter gauge so the tenon cut will be at the 5-inch line. Cut both sides of both ends with one pass each. Repeat for the second cross support. Remove the stop and clean out the rest of the tenons by continuing to move the piece so the blade is cutting closer to the end.

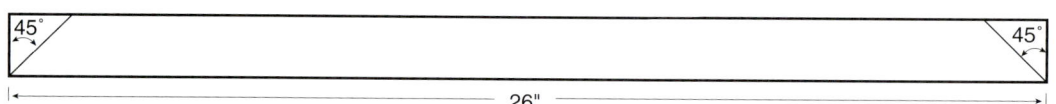

**Fig. 3**
**Cross Support Miters**

WALNUT & WENGE COFFEE TABLE

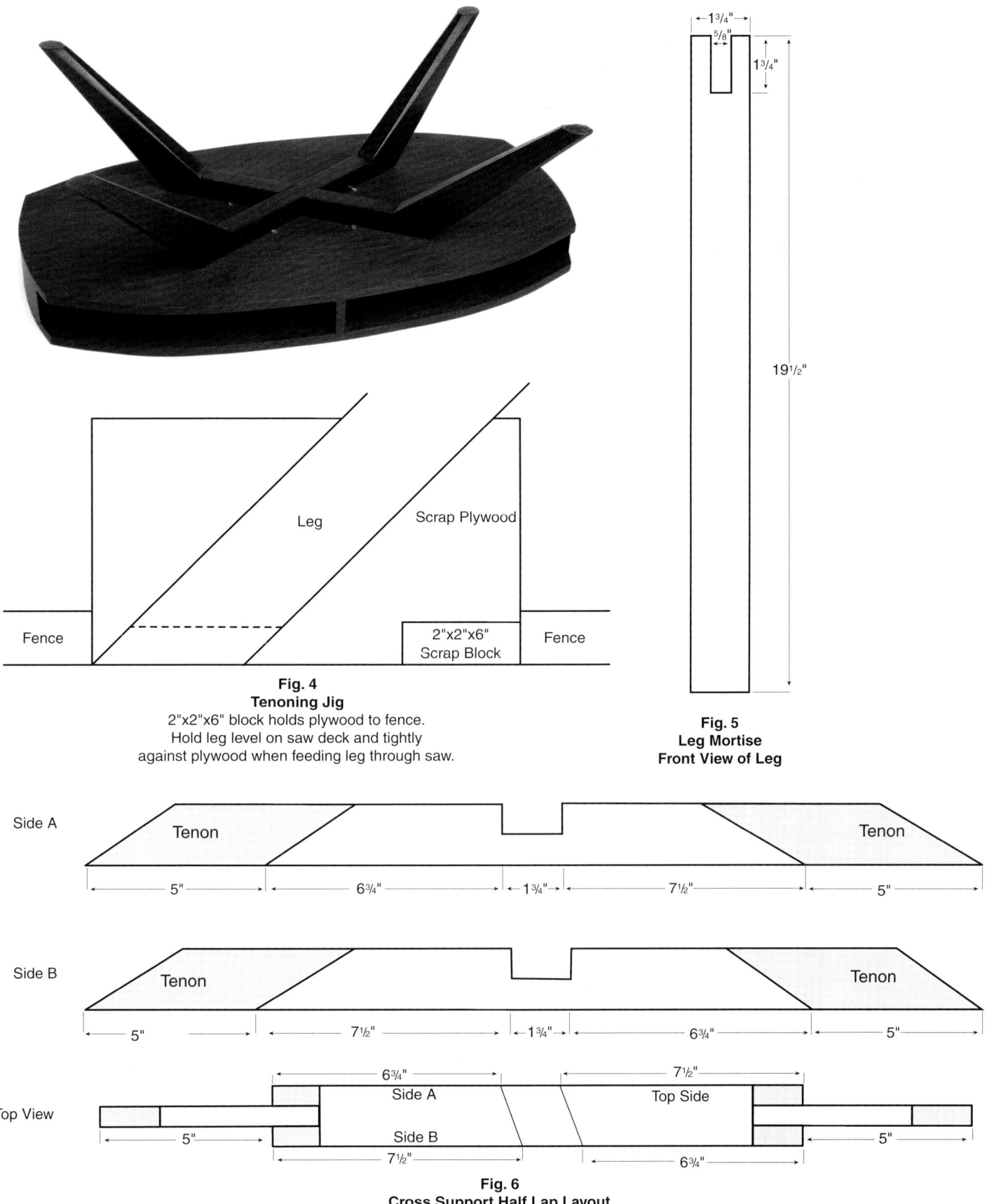

**Fig. 4
Tenoning Jig**
2"x2"x6" block holds plywood to fence.
Hold leg level on saw deck and tightly
against plywood when feeding leg through saw.

**Fig. 5
Leg Mortise
Front View of Leg**

**Fig. 6
Cross Support Half Lap Layout**

HOUSE OF WHITE BIRCHES, BERNE, INDIANA 46711   IN-STYLE ACCENT TABLES

5 For half laps, mark one side of each cross support with an A and the other side with a B. Measuring from the long point of the body of the cross support (excluding the tenon), mark the bottom of each cross support at 7½ inches on side A and 6¾ inches on side B; measure from the opposite end and mark 7½ inches on side B and 6¾ inches on side A (Fig. 6). Draw a line across the sides at these points to the top of each cross support, then draw connecting lines across the top and bottom (top view). Set one cross support on top of the other and verify that the angles and half-lap widths are correct. Set the dado height to ⅞ inch. Set the miter gauge to 65 degrees and a stop that allows the first cut to be on the inside of the 6¾-inch line. With the top side down on the first cross support, make one pass.

6 Take the other cross support; with the top side up, make one pass. Reset the stop to allow the cut to go to the inside of the second line. Make the pass with the cross support top-up. Move the cross support just enough to finish cleaning out the half-lap.

7 Make the second cut on the first cross support with the top down. Move the cross support just enough to finish cleaning out the half-lap. Trial-fit cross supports together.

### LEG TAPERS

1 Mark both sides of the bottom of each leg (D) 2¼ inches from the front edge. Carry the line across the bottom of the foot, using the combination square.

2 Draw a line across the back of the leg at the bottom of the mortise. Draw a line from the mortise line to the 2¼-inch line on each side of the leg.

3 Using the 7x30 inch plywood as a jig base and the 2x5-inch plywood fences, place the leg in the jig with the mortised end to the front. Align the mortise line with the edge of the jig base, and the 2¼-inch taper line with the base at the other end. Set the fences in place to hold the leg; secure fences to jig base with

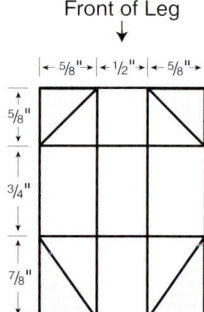

**Fig. 7**
**Bottom View of Leg**
Dark areas represent areas to be cut away.

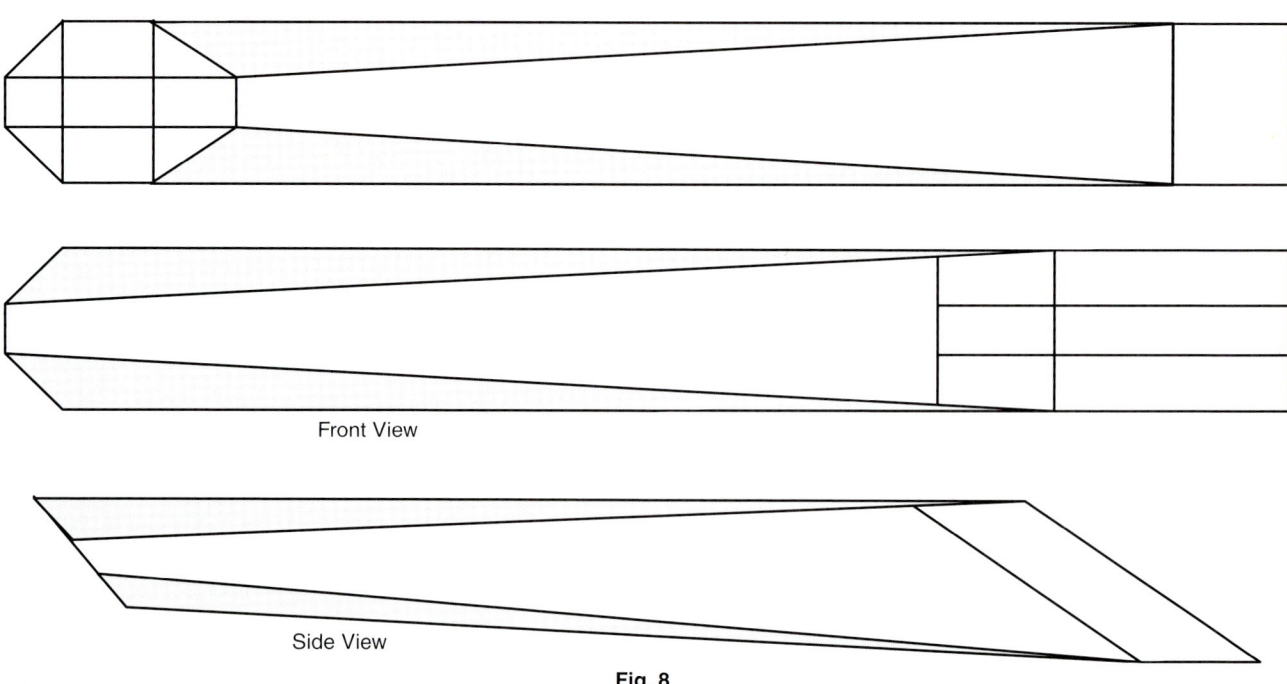

Front View

Side View

**Fig. 8**

1¼-inch screws. With the fence of the table saw set the width of the jig base from the blade, and the blade height at 2½ inches, cut the first taper on the leg. Repeat to cut the first taper on the remaining three legs.

**4** Referring to Fig. 7, mark the bottom of each foot, extending each mark slightly onto the sides of leg. Draw a line from each mark on the bottom back corners to the mortise line and on the front to the top of the leg (Fig. 8). Following these lines, shape the second taper on each leg using the shaping tool, as with the end uprights.

**5** Sand cross supports, avoiding the joint area and legs, to remove saw and shaping marks.

### ASSEMBLE & FINISH

**1** Glue two legs (D) to each cross support (E). Let dry. Glue cross supports together at half-lap joint, completing the base.

**2** Apply clear finish to base and unattached tabletop following manufacturer's instructions. Let dry thoroughly.

**3** Place table upside down on the work surface. Find and mark the centers on the table bottom and draw length and width lines indicating both.

**4** Drill eight ¾-inch holes ⅛ inch deep in the top of the table base—two in each cross piece and one on each side for the figure-eight fasteners. Attach one fastener in each hole, drilling a 1⁄16-inch pilot hole for each screw.

**5** Place the base upside down on the bottom of the tabletop, centering it over the top center lines. Secure base to table top with figure-eight fastener screws. ❈

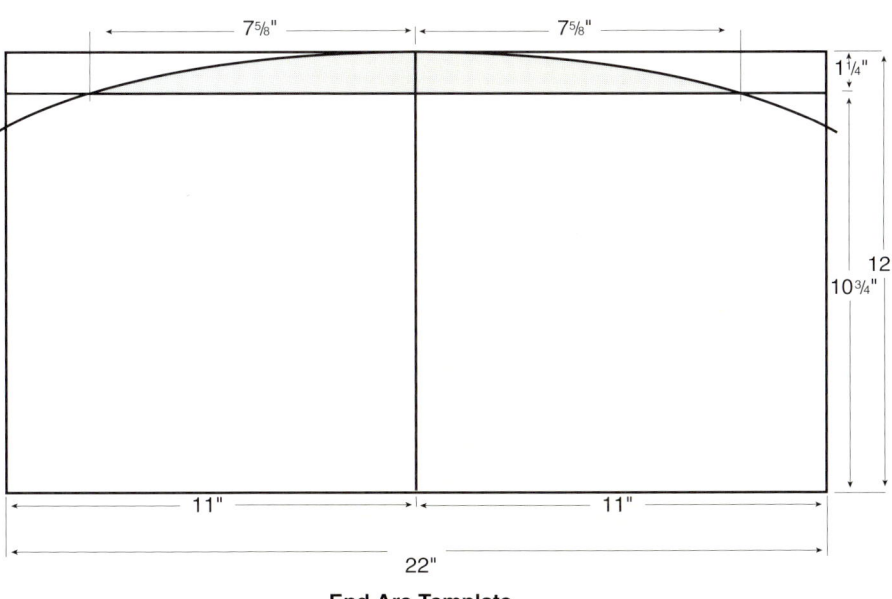

**End Arc Template**
Shaded area indicates final shape of end supports.

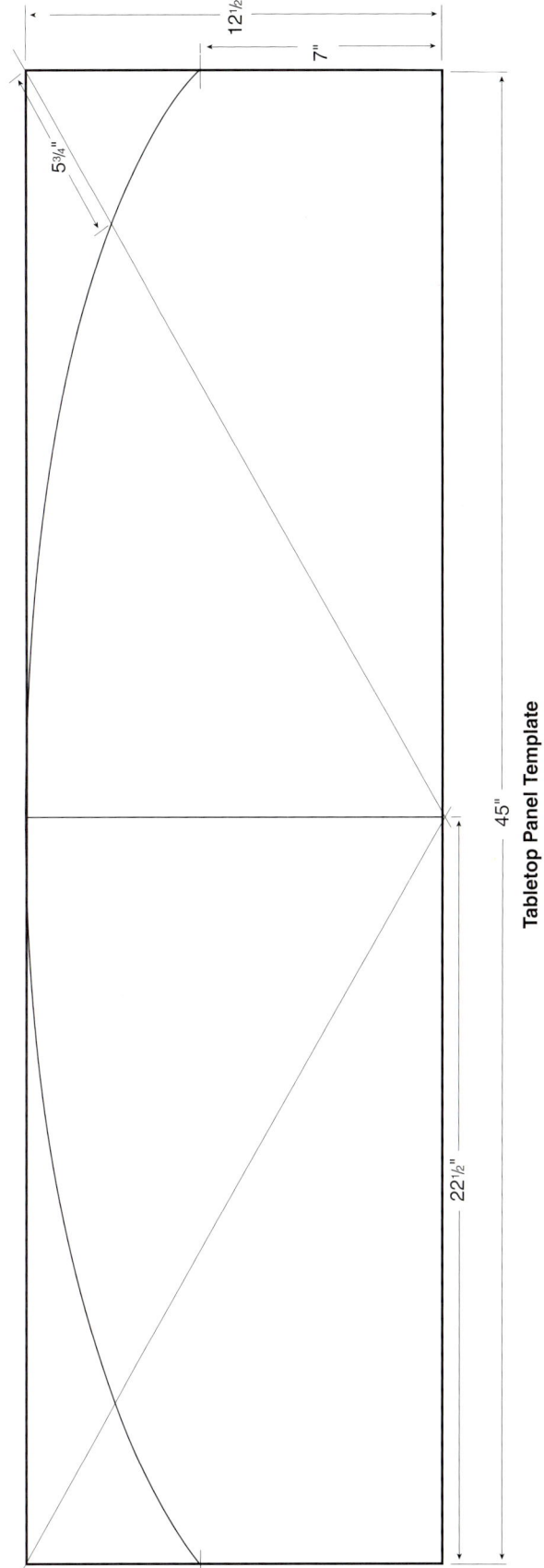

## Standard Lumber Dimensions

| NOMINAL | ACTUAL | METRIC |
|---|---|---|
| 1" x 2" | ¾" x 1½" | 19 x 38 mm |
| 1" x 3" | ¾" x 2½" | 19 x 64 mm |
| 1" x 4" | ¾" x 3½" | 19 x 89 mm |
| 1" x 5" | ¾" x 4½" | 19 x 114 mm |
| 1" x 6" | ¾" x 5½" | 19 x 140 mm |
| 1" x 7" | ¾" x 6¼" | 19 x 159 mm |
| 1" x 8" | ¾" x 7¼" | 19 x 184 mm |
| 1" x 10" | ¾" x 9¼" | 19 x 235 mm |
| 1" x 12" | ¾" x 11¼" | 19 x 286 mm |
| 2" x 3" | 1½" x 2½" | 38 x 64 mm |
| 2" x 4" | 1½" x 3½" | 38 x 89 mm |
| 2" x 6" | 1½" x 5½" | 38 x 140 mm |
| 2" x 8" | 1½" x 7¼" | 38 x 184 mm |
| 2" x 10" | 1½" x 9¼" | 38 x 235 mm |
| 2" x 12" | 1½" x 11¼" | 38 x 286 mm |
| 3" x 6" | 2½" x 5½" | 64 x 140 mm |
| 4" x 4" | 3½" x 3½" | 89 x 89 mm |
| 4" x 6" | 3½" x 5½" | 89 x 140 mm |

**Lumber is ordered by nominal size. Use this handy chart to convert project supply list (that are given in actual sizes) to lumber yard shopping list.**

Woodworking for Women™ is a trademark of DRG Texas LP, licensed for use by House of White Birches.

**In-Style Accent Tables** is published by House of White Birches, 306 East Parr Road, Berne, IN 46711, telephone (260) 589-4000. Printed in USA. Copyright © 2005 House of White Birches.

RETAILERS: If you would like to carry this pattern book or any other House of White Birches publications, call the Wholesale Department at Annie's Attic to set up a direct account: (903) 636-4303. Also, request a complete listing of publications available from House of White Birches.

Every effort has been made to ensure that the instructions in this pattern book are complete and accurate. We cannot, however, take responsibility for human error, typographical mistakes or variations in individual work.

**E-mail:** Customer_Service@whitebirches.com

**Staff**
**Editor:** Jeanne Stauffer
**Associate Editors:** Sue Reeves, Dianne Schmidt
**Assistant Art Director:** Nick Pierce
**Technical Editors:** Marla Freeman, Amy Phillips
**Copy Editors:** Michelle Beck, Conor Allen
**Graphic Arts Supervisor:** Ronda Bechinski
**Graphic Artists:** Allison Rothe, Shelley Muhlenkamp
**Photographers:** Christena Green, Carl Clark, Don Clark
**Photo Stylists:** Tammy Nussbaum, Tammy Smith

**ISBN:** 1-59635-004-0
1 2 3 4 5 6 7 8 9